Back ON Track

Boys Dealing With Sexual Abuse

By Leslie Bailey Wright &

Mindy B. Loiselle

SaferSocietyPress

PO BOX 340
BRANDON, VERMONT
05733-0340

Design: Sue Storey Design & Illustration

Editor: Euan Bear

Typesetting: Amy Rothstein, Pond Productions, Waltham, MA

Printing: Recycled Paper Printing, Inc. Boston, MA

ISBN: 1-884444-43-1
$14.00
Bulk discounts available.

Order from:

The Safer Society Press
P.O. Box 340
Brandon, VT 05733

802-247-3132

Phone orders welcome with
Visa or MasterCard.

Also available by Leslie Bailey Wright and Mindy Loiselle:
Shining Through: Pulling It Together After Sexual Abuse,
a workbook especially for girls ages 10 and up.

Acknowledgments

We would like to extend our sincere thanks to the boys and men who have shared their healing process with us. You taught us a great deal about the many paths healing can take. Additional thanks to the men who allowed us to interview them regarding their sexual abuse histories. We were touched by your courage, and we heard your hope that new young victims of sexual abuse will get the timely help they need.

We have been graced to be able to work again with our editor, Euan Bear. Her conviction, breadth of knowledge, and honesty add tremendously to the editorial dialogue and to this book. Her dedication to all survivors has been inspiring.

We thank our readers Olin McGill, Walter Zeichner, Stan Baker, Jon Conte and John Hunter for their comments and contributions. A special thank you to David Calof for his wonderful story.

Thanks to Jill Ward, Mark O'Shea, and Chris Bailey for your kind words and valued feedback. And as always, thanks to our husbands Randy and Lanny for their love and support.

About the Authors

Leslie Wright has worked in a variety of inpatient and outpatient settings as a licensed clinical social worker. She received her MSW from Virginia Commonwealth University in 1983. She now lives in Richmond with her husband and three children.

Mindy Loiselle is a licensed clinical social worker. She divides her professional time between her private practice and her work as a collateral assistant professor of social work at the Virginia Commonwealth University. Her personal time is spent with her husband, her labrador retriever, and her garden.

David Calof, author of the Introduction and the Last Word, is a family therapist in private practice in Seattle. A frequent lecturer and prolific author, he just released *The Couple Who Became Each Other* (Bantam Books), a casebook of healing tales culled from his 25 years as a practicing hypnotherapist.

Contents

Introduction   Hearing and Being Heard *by David Calof*   7

Chapter 1   So Where Do I Start?   11
How to Use this Book / Am I the Only One? / Who
Abuses? / It's Too Awful to Talk About! / When
You're Not Getting Support / Ways to Find Help /
Important Ideas

Chapter 2   Why Most Kids Don't Tell
(And What Happens When They Do)   23
Being Grounded / Couldn't Stop It Alone / Toughing
It Out / It's Too Weird! / What Will You Think About
Me? / How Other People Acted When They
Found Out / The Best Way People Can Help /
So What's Important Here?

Chapter 3   What If It Didn't Feel Like Abuse?   33
What Is Sexual Abuse? / Power / Knowledge Power /
Relationship Power / What About the Sexual Part? /
Why Talk About This? / Am I in Trouble Too? /
Important Ideas

Chapter 4   Sometimes You Know It Was Abuse   43
It Was Bad / Physical Power / Knowledge Power /
Relationship Power / Survival / What to Remember

Chapter 5   Sorting Out Feelings   49
Knowing More Helps / Feeling Guilty and Ashamed /
Feeling Alone / Feeling Angry / Feeling Sad / Feeling
Scared / Feeling Confused, Having Mixed Feelings /
Important Ideas

Chapter 6   Old Coping / New Coping 59
Coping / Separating Yourself from the Abuse / Just Not
Caring / Putting Anger in the Wrong Place / What Do I
Do Now? / Warning Signs / Getting
Help / Important Ideas

Chapter 7   Choosing Your Track 71
How Abuse Lowers Self-Esteem / Steps to Getting
Back on Your Track / Sexuality / Disconnecting
Sexuality from Abuse / Fears About Homosexuality /
Feeling Worried About My Body / Making Choices /
Important Ideas

Chapter 8   Therapy 85
I Don't Need Any Help! / I'll Figure It Out Myself! / I
Don't Want to Talk About It / What Therapy Should
Be Like / What Will I Do In Therapy? / What Will My
Therapist Tell Other People About Me? / Ways to Help
Your Therapist / What If I Hate It? / What's Important
Here?

Chapter 9   Now and Later 95
Your Family / When Your Family Won't or Can't
Help / Social Services / Courts / Relationship with the
Abuser / Relationship with the World / School and
Friends / Relationship with Yourself

In Closing   Staying on Track 109
A Safe Place / Motivation / Balance / Special Helpers /
Other Strengths / Turning Your Life into Something
Positive / An Important Special Message

Last Word   Luís and the Book of Hearing *by David Calof* 115

Hearing and Being Heard

If you're reading this book right now, I bet you've seen some pretty rough times. Once long ago I heard a tale about a boy named Luís, who also went through some tough times. This tale tells of the day that Luís read the Book of Hearing and what happened to him afterwards. Luís was a pretty special boy, but not more special than you are. You might like Luís, and I think Luís would probably like you. You can turn to the end of this book now, or maybe later on when you've read some more of this book, and read the story of Luís and the Book of Hearing. It's about hearing important things, and about being heard, even when you're not saying anything out loud. It's about hearing each other when we've been through tough stuff, and how we can help each other out, just by listening.

You probably don't know it yet, but this book you're reading right now is a part of the *Book of Hearing*. It isn't the *whole Book of Hearing*, but it's a pretty big part. This book probably ended up in your hands because some very bad things were done to you. Maybe even by people you loved and trusted. Afterwards these people probably told you to be quiet, to keep "our little secret," to never say anything about what they did to you. Then again, maybe you just plain felt so bad that you never wanted anyone to know.

Maybe at first you tried to tell people about the things that happened to you, but no one would hear you. After a while you probably even stopped hearing yourself when you cried. Then you probably stopped crying altogether. "Why bother?" you may have told yourself. "No one will hear anyway."

Yes they will.

This book will help people hear you when you talk about the things that happened to you. As part of the *Book of Hearing*, this book will even help you hear yourself, when the feelings you've tried to forget finally get heard and you start to cry again. Most of all, this book will help you understand what happened to you. Once you understand it, you'll know that *you never did anything to deserve these bad things.*

No grownups had the right to make you their "special friend." Grownups are supposed to find their special friends among people their own age, not among boys your age.

No older kids or kids your age had the right to steal by force, tricks, or bribes your choice of whether, when, or with whom you wanted to be sexual.

You had the right to find your special friends among boys and girls your own age. You also had the right to expect that the grown-ups around you would care for and protect you. You had the right to choose your own sexual partner when you were ready. If a grown-up or an older boy or girl, or even a group of kids your age stole any of these rights from you, then those people did something very, very wrong. As you work your way through this book, always remember that the people who took advantage of you are the ones who did something wrong. *Not you!*

I won't lie to you: There will be times when you'll want to throw this book right in the garbage, and never again think about what happened to you. You'll just want it all to go away and leave you alone. I understand why you would feel that way. So will the people around you, the ones who love you very much. They'll wish they had a magic wand, that they could wave it over your head and make it all just go away for you.

But it won't just go away. Whenever we've been badly hurt, especially by people we love and trust, we always have to talk about it sooner or later, or we never get over it. I want you to think about what I'm going to say. Think really *really* hard, because this point is worth more than all the video games in the world. Remember a time when you felt bad about something that happened to you *out in the open.* Maybe your "best" friend made up a lie about you. Maybe no one paid much attention to you when you got 4 A's and 1 B, because your sister got all A's. Remember how much *better* you felt after you talked it all out with a friend or a brother or a teacher?

That's *just* how we usually go about making ourselves feel better when we've been hurt. We bring it out into the open, talk about how we feel, pull ourselves together, and figure out how to get back on track. Then we get along to the next adventure coming our way.

But you probably never had the chance to talk to anyone about the terrible things that happened to you. At least not until now. Don't worry if you find it pretty hard at first to talk about the things that were done to you. These things are hard for boys to talk about. They're even hard for grown-ups to talk about. But hang in there, and keep talking about them. Above all, remember this: *Just because people seem embarrassed and unsure of themselves when you talk about the things that happened to you, don't **ever** think that you did something to deserve it.* You didn't.

As you turn the page and begin to read this book, I want you always to remember that it's a part of the *Book of Hearing*. And Luís says to tell you that, if anyone asks what you're doing, just tell them you're writing a report on the ear.

David Calof, Editor Emeritus
Treating Abuse Today
Seattle, Washington

Chapter 1

So Where Do I Start?

Something happened. Since then you may have wondered about it and thought things like "How can things get so screwed up?" and "Why me?" and "It isn't fair!"

If you've ever wondered any of these things about being sexually abused, you're not alone. And you're right — it isn't fair. Sexual abuse never is.

Because it did happen, the most important question is how to deal with it in a way that gets your life back on the track you want it to be on. The truth is, being sexually abused bumps boys off the track they were on. Getting your life heading back in the direction you choose will take work. You'll need help along the way, but most of the work only you can do.

In a way, you can compare sexual abuse to getting an injury, let's say breaking your arm in a backyard football game. It wasn't your fault. But if you want to get better and get back in the game, several things will need to happen.

In this case it's easy to see that you'll need help from others: the person who calls the ambulance or drives you to the emergency room, the X-ray technician, the nurse and the doctor who will set the bone and put the cast on it, physical therapists and friends. Without that help, the bone wouldn't heal correctly, and you might have scars.

But even with the right medical help, you'll have to work to get your arm back in shape, as strong as it can be.

While it may not be as clear with sexual abuse, not doing what needs to be done can leave injuries and scars, even if you can't see them. Not dealing with sexual abuse can leave you with injuries to your thoughts and feelings.

The good news is that, like fixing the broken arm, healing from sexual abuse is possible. But, just like the broken arm, it takes time, help from others, and mostly your hard work.

We believe you're reading this book now because you've made a decision about healing. You may want to know more about sexual abuse, why it happens, and who it happens to. Maybe you'd like to better understand your own reactions to the abuse, or perhaps you're looking for ideas on how to deal better with what's happened. Or it could be that you're reading this book because someone who knows what happened thought you might be interested. Whatever your reason for choosing to read this book, we hope it gives you some of the help and information you need.

How to Use this Book

We know that a big problem with sexual abuse is that most people don't know how to talk about it. And, we know that even when you do feel ready to talk, it can be hard to find the words you want. We wrote this book to make finding the words you want a little easier. In our work with sexually abused boys, we have seen how much it helped when they could find the words for their thoughts and feelings about being abused.

Feel free to read this book in a way that works best for you. We believe it's best if you have an adult to share your ideas with. If an adult gave you this book, he or she may be a good person to start talking with. Other possibilities include teachers, guidance counselors, family members, or a sponsor from a 12-Step program. If you don't have anyone you trust to help you at this point, you'll find a section on "Some Ways to Find Help" later in this chapter.

At the end of each chapter, you'll find something called "Your Turn." Here you'll find some suggestions and written exercises. These exercises, along with the information in the chapters, are there to help you to:

1. learn more about how sexual abuse has affected your life;

2. figure out what it is you want to do about it; and

3. learn skills that can help you feel more in control of the situation.

It won't happen overnight, or even in a few months, but eventually you can feel better. And then you'll be back on track for getting where it is *you* want to go in life.

Am I the Only One?

No! Unfortunately, sexual abuse of boys and girls happens all too often. And it happens in all parts of the world, to boys and girls from all races and religions, and to those from all types of families — rich, poor, and in-between. Statistics (a fancy way of counting) tell us that thousands of boys are abused each year.[1]

Therapists and counselors have learned a lot about how boys feel after sexual abuse from talking to men who were abused when they were young. Most of these men never told anyone about the abuse until they were grown. Many have talked about how alone and different they felt because of the abuse, and how they believed the abuse was their own fault. Each of these men remembers questioning whether or not he was "a real man" after the abuse, but there was no one to talk to about these worries.

Now, as men, they are learning that the abuse was *not* their fault and that they never deserved to feel bad about themselves. They've now learned that no matter what happened, or what anybody said, their manhood was not taken away by being abused. Many of these men wish that they could have learned these things while they were younger, and they are glad to know that more and more boys are now getting the help they need and deserve.

Who Abuses?

neighbor	uncle	mother	brother	stepparent
father	minister	babysitter	camp counselor	aunt
teacher	cousin	family friend	friend's parent	coach
sister	grandparent	stranger	your friend	friend's friend

Most people do not sexually abuse kids, but you can't tell by who they are or what job they do whether they might be sexually abusive. Unfortunately, people who sexually abuse usually don't look or act any different from other people, until it comes to sexual touching. There is no way to know just by looking who can be abusive. Sometimes kids are abused by more than one person.

---

[1] Finkelhor, David. *Child Sexual Abuse: New Theory and Research*. New York: Free Press, 1984.

While some boys are abused by strangers, most are abused by someone they know. Boys can be abused by either men or women, older boys or girls. Some abusers are married and have what everyone else sees as a "normal" life. Many boys are abused by a teenager.

Most abusers sexually abuse more than one kid. More than likely, you were not the only one.

It's Too Awful to Talk About!

Dealing with sexual abuse sometimes means thinking and talking about difficult stuff. Most kids — and adults, too — find it tough and embarrassing to talk about sexual abuse, especially at first. If your experience is like many of the boys and girls we've worked with, there may be times when sexual abuse feels too awful to deal with. At these times you may want to feel and act like it never happened, or relate to it as if it happened to someone else, or think that what happened wasn't that bad. While it might be hard to believe now, most kids find that it gets easier to deal with as time goes on. Many guys have found that talking about what happened can even feel good at times. It can help them feel less alone. So even if you feel awful at first, try to stay with it.

Here are some ideas that may help you when you feel stuck.

1. Pacing Yourself
It takes a lot of time and work to deal with being sexually abused. However, that doesn't mean you shouldn't have breaks, time to relax, and to have fun. Everyone needs breaks from the hard stuff once in awhile. For some kids, making friends, relaxing, and having fun don't come naturally. If that's true for you, you can change it if you want to. Make it a goal and then get the help you need to make some changes in your life. We know that "learning how to have fun" can sound a bit strange as a goal at first, but it isn't really. Friends, fun, and relaxation are important parts of life, and everyone needs and deserves them.

2. Accepting that Sometimes You Feel Worse
  Before You Can Feel Better
There is no good way to deal with being sexually abused without having some painful feelings and thoughts. Sometimes, really looking at the hard stuff is what needs to be done to get better in the long run.

At these times, it's extra important that you have people you can trust to help you through it.

3. Getting More Support

The easiest way to feel ready to talk about difficult stuff like sexual abuse is by having enough support. Support comes from people who care about you and who try to understand when you feel bad, people who really listen to you. Support comes from people who can remind you that you are a good, strong, capable person who happens to be having a hard time dealing with tough stuff.

All of us need people we can go to when we're feeling confused, bad, or shaky, though a lot of guys find it hard to ask for help and support. Asking for help shows real strength, strength of mind, spirit, and character. Getting help doesn't mean you're not strong. Strong people need and deserve help too. If you have a therapist or counselor as one of your helpers, that's great, but he or she cannot be there all the time. It's best when you're able to get support from several people.

When You're Not Getting Support

There are times when a kid is abused by a family member or even by someone outside the family, and other family members don't believe it or blame the kid. Some family members or friends might believe you and others might not. When family members don't believe you about the abuse, counselors say the family is "in denial." This is another way of saying the family cannot or will not face the truth. Family denial usually makes the boy or girl feel worse than ever, but it's not his or her fault. Kids can't stop other people's denial.

If your family is in denial, it is especially important that you find someone else you can trust, someone who believes in you. Although it makes everything harder when you don't have the support of family members, you can continue working on making things better for yourself.

Other people outside the family may also be in denial and not believe what you tell them about being sexually abused. In fact a lot of people can't accept the fact that boys are sexually abused. Others know really well that boys are abused and can face the truth. We hope you have supportive people who believe you. Some people might be in denial at first, but later they can listen and give you the support you deserve.

If you're getting what you need from your family, then it sounds like your family is on the road to making things better for everyone. If no one in your family can or will help, here are steps you can take to get the support you need and deserve. Keep trying!

Ways to Find Help

1. Think about who might help you.
Is there a teacher, guidance counselor, friend, neighbor, family member, or other adult who is nice to you in a way that feels good, who respects you, who does what they say they will do? Tell that person what's going on. If you think it would help, show them this section of the book. If that person does not help, don't give up. Remember, you deserve help. Start thinking about another person who might help.

2. Tell your caseworker or therapist what's really going on.
We know it can be hard to trust others with such important information. You may be scared about what's going to happen if you tell someone you are not being protected or helped in your family. Still, your caseworker or therapist cannot help you or your family unless he or she knows what is really happening. Remember, it's not your job to protect grownups. We know that *saying* this and *feeling* it are two different things. Often, it takes a long time and a lot of thinking about it, feeling about it, and help with it to really let this sink in. It's you're right to do all you can to protect yourself.

3. If you don't have a caseworker or therapist, call Social Services or Child Protection.
Each city, county, or town should have a number in the phone book you can call to ask questions or to ask for help. It's usually listed under "Social Services." Or you can call Child Help USA. The number is 1-800-4ACHILD or 1-800-422-4453. Calling won't cost anything (and it won't show up on anyone's phone bill — you can even call from a pay phone). They can answer some of your questions and can tell you where to find help in your own area.

Important Ideas

- Sexual abuse can leave you with injuries to your thoughts and feelings.

- Getting better takes time, plenty of attention, and help from others.

- Everyone needs a break sometimes. Take time to relax and have fun.

- You deserve help in dealing with this. Getting help doesn't mean a person isn't strong. Strong people need and deserve help too.

Your Turn

Dealing with sexual abuse is a tough job. Sometimes it can all feel like too much. How do you know when you're feeling overloaded? List some of the ways you can tell that you're stressed out and need help and/or a break.

Example

1. I can't concentrate on my schoolwork and have trouble falling asleep.

2. I have nightmares about the abuse.

_____

_____

_____

_____

_____

Have other people pointed out things that you do that make them believe you are stressed out?

Example

John's teacher told his mother that John looked angry all the time at school lately.

Has anyone said you look angry or out of it or stressed? Write down what other people have pointed out about you.

_____

_____

_____

_____

_____

_____

A *plan* is when you figure out the steps of what you need to do to get something to happen. If you want to go to a particular movie, step one of your plan would be looking up where the movie is playing and at what time. In step two you would check to see if you have enough money for the roundtrip bus fare and the movie ticket. In step three you would find out the bus schedule and leave your house in time to get to the bus stop. Step four is to catch the bus that'll stop at the theater before the show starts. Step five is to buy your ticket and go into the theater. If you wanted to ask a friend to go with you, calling your friend and setting a time and place to meet would be another step in your plan for going to the movies.

Having a fire drill at school is another kind of plan, a plan for what to do in an emergency: how people will be told there's an emergency, the best way to get organized so no one is left behind, which stairs and doors each group will take, where to meet outside, and who will count to make sure everyone is out of the building.

Just like going to the movies or having a fire drill at school, you can make a plan for how to deal with being stressed out. Part of your plan might be about how you'll know that you're stressed out and need to put the plan into action! Think about what you might do to help yourself feel better — like shooting hoops, swimming, hitting a baseball, or finding someone to talk to — or how you can get some help from other important people in your life.

Write down your plan for what you can do the next time you are feeling stressed out.

Sample Plan

1. Notice when I'm spacing out and making excuses not to be with people.

2. Get my parents to read this section of the book.

3. Tell someone who cares about me that I'm stressed out and ask him or her for ideas on how to get unstressed.

4. Give myself a break. Call a friend to go to the movies.

Your Plan

1. _____

2. _____

3. _____

4. _____

5. _____

6. _____

What are some ways you relax and have fun?

_____

_____

_____

Can you list some new ways to relax and have fun that you'd like to learn or try?

_____

_____

_____

_____

_____

_____

_____

_____

_____

Your Space

At the end of each chapter, you'll find a "your space" page or two. This is a place for you to use in any way that works for you. You can jot down some notes, write down your reactions to what you've read, or do some drawing. Some people express themselves more easily with pictures than with words. Don't be critical of your work. Feel free to do anything you want. Lots of people find that using color helps them express themselves.

Your Space

Chapter 2

Why Most Kids
Don't Tell
(And What Happens When They Do)

A lot of sexually abused kids don't tell anyone that they are being abused. The fact that a guy doesn't tell anyone can be confusing for some people. We know that boys (and girls) may not tell for awhile for a lot of different reasons. Do any of these ideas remind you of what was happening to you?

Being Grounded

A lot of boys were sexually abused when they were doing something away from home. Sometimes they weren't supposed to be where they were, or they weren't supposed to be there alone. If a boy was molested when he was hanging out some place (whether he was supposed to be there or not), he may be afraid of getting in trouble. His parents might say, "No friends over, no parties, no hanging out. You go to school and then you come home, and that's it." So he never tells his parents that he was abused because he is afraid he will be grounded and lose his freedom. A parent might see this as a way to protect a kid from dangerous people, but to the kid it feels like being punished.

Example

Shakeel was at the mall alone when he wasn't supposed to be. A man called him over to a phone booth and asked if he had any change. When he put his hand in his pocket, the man grabbed Shakeel's crotch. Shakeel pulled away and ran toward a group of people. He never told anyone until years later.

Another way to think about it . . .

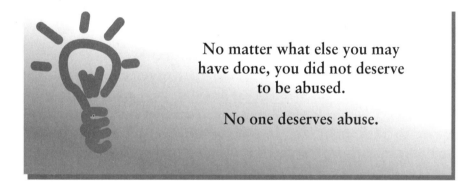

No matter what else you may have done, you did not deserve to be abused.

No one deserves abuse.

Couldn't Stop It Alone

Some guys think they should handle everything by themselves all the time. When something big like sexual abuse happens, a boy can get really angry at himself for not being able to stop it. He thinks he can't tell anyone about it because they'd think he was a wimp, a baby. Actually, sexual abuse is REALLY hard to stop by yourself.

Example

George, aged 17, had been sort of roughhousing with Jamal, his 12-year-old neighbor. He would pull Jamal to him and grab his butt. A few times he even hit Jamal, although he said he was just "kidding around." George kept adding more sexual things, like grabbing at Jamal's crotch. He even made Jamal do him "favors" like giving him money. Jamal kept getting angry at himself for not stopping George. He tried walking home from school a different way for a few days, but George followed him the next day. He made fun of Jamal and said, "you'll never get away from me!"

Another way to think about it . . .

Needing help doesn't mean you're not strong! Even strong people need help sometimes!

Toughing It Out

We all get lots of messages from TV shows, movies, videos, and songs about what it means to be "a man." The idea is that acting "like a man" means certain things, including handling everything yourself and not showing any feelings except anger. By the time they are in school, a lot of guys have come to believe that they can't tell anyone when they have a problem, that they just need to be tough. "Toughing it out" becomes a way of life for a lot of kids. We bet you can remember a time when you hurt yourself, and when you cried someone said, "Don't be a baby." So when something like sexual abuse happens, many boys believe the best way to handle it is to "tough it out."

Example

John knew that his dad had been in his older sister Lauren's room a bunch of times, and he could hear her crying afterwards. As John got older, he began to realize that something sexual was happening. When his dad started coming to his bed and doing sexual things, he decided, "Lauren can take it, so I can take it, too."

Another way to think about it . . .

Being tough doesn't mean not telling. Some of the toughest kids we know used their toughness to tell someone they were being abused.

It's Too Weird!

More is written and said in public about sexual abuse than ever before. However, most of the talk is about girls and sexual abuse. Some people even think sexual abuse doesn't happen to boys. While some boys have heard that it happens to boys, they've never heard about the way it happened to them. One example is if a guy is sexually abused by a woman, such as his mother, a babysitter, an aunt or his grandmother, he may think it's "too weird" to talk about. He might even think that no one would believe him.

Example

Charles' aunt came to visit and said that she was too cold at night to sleep alone. When she got into bed with him, he was mad. In the middle of the night, he felt her reach out and touch his penis. He felt really trapped and never told anyone.

If a boy is abused by a woman outside his family, like a neighbor or an older teenager, he may be confused about what it means. He may have heard that all sexual contact with a woman is supposed to feel good. If he did not like the experience, he may worry that other people will think he's strange or "not a real man" or that he's gay.

Another way to think about it . . .

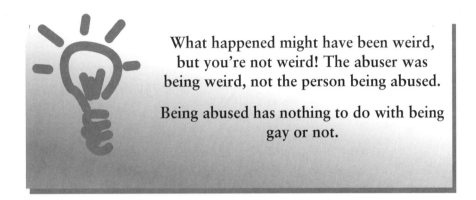

What happened might have been weird, but you're not weird! The abuser was being weird, not the person being abused.

Being abused has nothing to do with being gay or not.

What Will You Think About Me?

We all have ideas about how we want people to see us and how we want to feel about ourselves. All of us want to be liked and to have people think we are okay.

Boys often wonder if they are okay or not after the sexual abuse has happened. They often think that sexual abuse will mean that other people will think they are *not* okay. Because a boy has these ideas, he often doesn't want anybody to find out about the sexual abuse.

Even "everyday" sexual things are generally hard to talk about for a lot of people. It's that much harder to find people who may feel comfortable talking about sexual abuse. When you wanted to talk about it, it might have been hard to think of a person who would understand. That's why it's important that you have a person (or better still, a few people) you feel okay talking to about it now. They can remind you that you are an okay person, that your pain and confusion about the abuse is a normal reaction, and that you can get through this.

Another way to think about it . . .

> No matter what, no matter if a man molested you or a woman, no matter if you thought it was abuse or not, no matter if you liked what they did or not . . . you are still a boy, a young man, and will someday be a man. Nothing can change that.

How Other People Acted When They Found Out

Sexual abuse is hard to understand for the person it's happening to. It's usually hard to understand for other people too — even people who should help right away. No matter how other people found out about your being abused, we hope they knew what to do and how to help. A lot of times, it doesn't happen that way. If people didn't know how to help, they probably acted one of these ways.

SHOCKED — Some people act like being sexually abused was the most horrible thing that could ever happen. If the person you told was shocked, you might wonder if you'll ever be okay again.

SCARED / WORRIED — Maybe the person you told looked very worried and asked you lots of questions. Often people ask questions you don't know the answers to, like, "Why did he do that?" If the person you told seemed scared or worried, you may feel more worried.

ANGRY — Parents sometimes act really mad when they find out their son was sexually abused. They start yelling — they yell at the boy, they yell about the person who molested him. If your parents were upset and yelled, you might have felt like you did something bad, or like the abuse was your fault, or that you made them feel bad.

SILENCE — Even though sexual abuse is talked about now, most people think it will NEVER happen to someone they know. So when it does happen, they just don't know how to act, and then they do nothing. When this happens, it can be pretty confusing. If this is how people around you reacted, you probably weren't sure what they were thinking. You may have wondered if they even cared. You might have wondered if what happened to you was too awful to talk about.

SADNESS — Being sexually abused is lousy. It shouldn't happen to anyone. It's a tough thing, but lots of people get through it and heal from it. If people around you get super sad, you might wonder if they know something you don't, and if things are going to get REALLY bad. You may feel upset because you think you caused their sadness by telling them.

BLAMING — Sometimes people want someone to blame when bad things happen. If the people around you were feeling this way, they may have blamed you for sexual abuse. Sometimes the blame comes out through angry questions like "Why did you let him do that?" or "Why did you go with her?" These questions are often too hard, too complicated to answer. If people blamed you, you probably felt really upset.

The Best Way People Can Help

The best way people can help when they find out is to say:

1. Being sexually abused is not your fault.

2. The other person MUST be stopped from molesting you ever again.

3. You have really earned my respect by being brave enough to tell me.

4. Being molested is a really bad break, but you can get through this and your life can get back on track.

5. That must be really tough on you. How can I help?

It's never too late to learn better ways of helping yourself or others. Show the people you want help from this section of the book. Many people in your life may really want to help. They just don't know how. If you are in therapy, tell your therapist how the other people in your life are acting. He or she can help you and your helpers figure out what to do.

So What's Important Here?

- You probably were unsure whether or not to tell about sexual abuse.

- You're not alone. A lot of kids get sexually abused. Many kids don't tell at first.

- You deserve help. If people don't know how to help yet, they can learn.

Your Turn

How did people around you act when they found out about your being sexually abused? Pick one person at a time and think about each one. Write here what they said and did:

1. Name _____

   How they acted: _____

   _____

2. Name _____

   How they acted: _____

   _____

3. Name _____

   How they acted: _____

   _____

4. Name _____

   How they acted: _____

Most guys have ideas about how they wished it had been when they told. Write here about the way you wished it had been for you.

_____

_____

_____

_____

_____

_____

_____

_____

_____

_____

_____

_____

_____

Your Space

Chapter 3

What If
It Didn't Feel Like Abuse?

M any kids are confused about the idea of "sexual abuse."
They don't feel "abused." A lot of kids do feel abused, and
we'll talk about their experiences more in the next chapter.
But some kids reject the idea that what happened was "abuse," and
they say things like this:

> I don't feel abused! I really liked the guy / the lady. He / She
> was really good to me and I don't think he / she would try
> to hurt me. That can't be abuse!

If you feel like you weren't abused, you are probably upset that
people think that you were. You might even be reading this book
because someone else thinks you should. Here is why they think it was
probably abuse — it has to do with one word — POWER.

What Is Sexual Abuse?

Sexual abuse is defined in different ways, depending on who is
talking — a lawyer or a therapist. In courts of law, legal definitions
are used. Legal definitions of sexual abuse are different in different
states. Proving in a court of law that a person was sexually abused by
another person is often difficult. Going to court may be necessary, and
sometimes it's even emotionally helpful when you've been abused. But
legal definitions and procedures are not often the best measure of the
pain and confusion caused by sexual abuse.

So what is sexual abuse? Whenever a kid is tricked, forced, bribed,
or threatened into sexual behavior of any kind by someone who has
more power, it is sexual abuse. Many abusers "trick" kids with
niceness by giving little kids candy, bigger kids money or special
favors. Any sexual contact an adult has with a child or teenager is
legally considered abuse.

Sexual abuse is not about whether you liked it or not. It has to do with one person using his or her power over you to do sexual things.

Power

Power can mean a lot of things. The first thing people tend to think about is **physical power** — who can push who around. But there are other equally important kinds of power. We all have **personal power** — beliefs about what's right and wrong and the ability to speak up about our beliefs. We can also get power from other people around us who will help us if we are in trouble.

Sexual abuse happens when one person misuses his or her power over another person. This can happen in a number of ways. The easiest to imagine is through physical power, but there are other ways power is used to allow the sexual abuse to occur.

Knowledge Power

A person who has experience can often talk someone else into doing something they may not really want to do. Abusers are often experts at doing this. They can make the other person feel stupid about saying no. Or they might back a younger or less experienced person into a corner where saying no doesn't feel possible. Words have a lot of power. Some boys may not have known enough about sexual behaviors to know that anything unusual was going on. The abuser used his or her knowledge to trick the boy.

Example

Raymond, who was 9, had become friends with his 18-year-old sister's boyfriend, Jim. When they were wrestling in Raymond's room, Jim said, "Let me show you something," and took out his penis. Raymond felt unsure and wanted him to stop. Jim said, "What are you afraid of?" and Raymond didn't know what to say. Jim said, "You'll really like this, just put your hand on it." Raymond didn't know how to say that he didn't want to, so he did it. He didn't want Jim to think he was a baby. Later Jim said, "I knew you wanted to." Raymond felt tricked and trapped.

Relationship Power

A lot of people have power in our lives because of their relationship to us, like an older brother or sister, for example. A teacher or a coach is another example. When you are in a relationship with someone you care about or depend on or admire, you may do things that they encourage you to do that you may never have done on your own. You do it because you trust that this person wouldn't try to hurt you or make you do something that was bad for you. Or, you do it because you're afraid they won't like you or they will say something bad about you to other people.

What About the Sexual Part?

We'll talk more about the "sexual" part later, but for now you need to know that "sexual" acts are any one of many behaviors that people do to get sexual pleasure. That covers lots of behavior. Don't forget that what gives one person pleasure, another person might not like at all. Also, what feels good with one person may feel awful with a different person. But if you don't think what happened was abuse at all, maybe the sexual part was something that you liked.

Example

Alex was 10 when his 17-year old cousin Sarah began to rub his penis when she was staying with his family. He felt pretty cool that she was doing such grownup sexual stuff with him. Over the next two years they got together as much as they could, and eventually they had intercourse. When Sarah went off to college, she got involved in sexual relationships with guys there. When Alex found out, he was depressed and angry. His favorite teacher asked him what was wrong one day after school, and Alex bitterly told him, "My girlfriend is screwing other guys." With a few more questions, the teacher discovered that the girlfriend was Alex's much older cousin and that the relationship had been going on for years. Alex was shocked when his teacher said he would have to report it as "abuse."

When a person who has power uses it to do a sexual act with another person who doesn't have as much power, that is abuse. Even if the less powerful person liked it or liked the more powerful person, it is still abuse because of the misuse of power and knowledge to get sex. Here are some other examples. Are any of them like your experience?

Nine-year-old Kaleb has been hanging around his friend Greg's house for awhile. One day when he went over, Greg wasn't there, but Greg's 16-year-old sister La Tonya and her girlfriend were. They asked him up to La Tonya's bedroom to play some music and then got him to do a strip dance where he pulled down his pants. They played with his penis, and when he got an erection, they tried to put his penis inside of their vaginas. It didn't work real well, but they said that they would "make him a man" and he liked that.

Kaleb felt proud and important that La Tonya and her friends thought he could be a man so soon. But at the same time, he was secretly embarrassed that it didn't work, and he wasn't sure that doing a strip dance was something a man would do. The girls had laughed some, and he felt more like a pet or a mascot than a man. There were other confusing feelings he just didn't know how to talk about.

Jamie (15) and Zack (10) have been in foster care together for six months. Zack is really angry to be there. He misses his dad, he doesn't like the foster family, and he hates his new school. He often can't sleep at night and lays in bed wide awake. For the last two months, Jamie has been coming to his bed and getting Zack to suck his penis. Zack thought this was pretty weird and kind of gross, but it was nice to have Jamie in his bed.

Having John come to him for physical contact helped Zack feel less lonely in foster care. Zack didn't really want to do the sexual stuff but because it helped him feel less lonely, he didn't try to stop it.

Paul (12) has been on the swim team for two years. His coach always kidded around with the other team members, but he gave a little more attention to Paul. Paul noticed that the coach would lean against him or touch his shoulder or arm. Usually it felt good, and he noticed that the coach had been doing it more lately. One day the coach kept Paul late after practice, and the coach had put his arm around him to explain how important it was for Paul to trust him and do what he said during swim meets. As they were standing there together, feeling kind of close, the coach reached over and put his hand on Paul's penis. It felt kind of nice, like part of being close.

Paul admired his coach just like the other kids did. He felt really special that the coach was spending more time with him than with the others. Paul had noticed that the coach treated him differently, and when the coach started touching him sexually, it was a little weird, a little uncomfortable, but it also made him feel special and important, like the coach trusted him. That's a hard feeling to give up.

Why Talk About This?

One difficult thing about sexual abuse is how confusing it is, especially if you like the person or liked the feeling. This confusion might be made up of many feelings: surprise, fear, pleasure, anger, uneasiness, loneliness, and feeling trapped are some of the feelings we hear about. Sometimes boys don't really like the sexual part, but they do like other parts of the relationship with the person who abused them. They feel shocked that other people think of the person as "abusive." It doesn't feel that clear to the boy. When other people think that he or she was wrong, the boy may want to defend the person.

Another confusing situation is if the boy liked the sexual part, but didn't like the person he was sexual with. That situation may still not seem like "abuse." The boy may think that because he was sexually involved it's not fair to say that the abuser was wrong. But the part that is wrong is that the person used their power to get the boy to do sexual things. Sometimes it's hard to remember about power. Sometimes it especially tough for a guy to admit that he wasn't as powerful as the person who sexually molested him.

Am I In Trouble Too?

It's back to that idea about power. We know you have your own power, but in this situation, the abuser had more power. When the abuser used that power to be sexual with you, the abuser was wrong, not you. If you were to misuse your power to take advantage of someone else sexually or in another way, or if some of the ways you cope with feelings are hurting yourself or others, that's wrong, too. But you did not deserve to be abused, and the abuse was not your fault.

Important Ideas

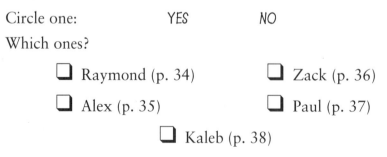

- The idea of sexual abuse is confusing to most kids.

- Sexual abuse involves the misuse of power.

- Some kids like some parts of the relationship with the person who abused them and not other parts.

Your Turn

Did any of the examples in this chapter remind you of what happened to you?

Circle one: YES NO

Which ones?

❑ Raymond (p. 34)   ❑ Zack (p. 36)

❑ Alex (p. 35)   ❑ Paul (p. 37)

❑ Kaleb (p. 38)

If you think that what happened to you was not sexual abuse, write here why you think so.

_____

_____

_____

_____

_____

_____

If you were confused about whether or not you were abused, what things felt like abuse and what things didn't? What were the bad parts of what was done to you? What were the good parts of what happened?

_____

_____

_____

_____

_____

_____

_____

_____

If it happened to a friend of yours or another kid, how would you feel about it?

_____

_____

_____

_____

_____

_____

Here are some ideas we've heard from boys who don't think that they were sexually abused. Check ones that you agree with.

❑ It was fun.

❑ It wasn't too bad.

❑ He wouldn't hurt me.

❑ I never said no.

❑ It didn't hurt.

❑ I don't want her to get in trouble.

❑ I thought he liked me.

❑ She's my friend.

❑ It had happened already with someone else.

❑ It's important to learn about sex.

❑ It felt good.

❑ It hurt, but I asked for it.

❑ Everyone does it sometimes.

❑ It made me feel like a man.

❑ Sex is just one of those secret things that grown-ups don't want us kids to do. I did it and I'm proud of it.

❑ I had to do it to prove I could.

❑ I wanted to do it to get into the gang.

Write any ideas you had that weren't listed.

_____

_____

_____

_____

_____

_____

_____

Your Space

Chapter 4

Sometimes You Know It Was Abuse

Some abusers, like the ones we talked about in the last chapter, trick kids into being sexual by being nice to them. They may buy the kid presents, and spend special time together doing fun things like going to baseball games, concerts, camping, or fishing. But others aren't nice at all. Some start out nice and then turn mean. They may use threats, punishment or force to make kids do sexual things. They don't really care much what the kid thinks or feels. They just want to have power and make other people do what they want.

It Was Bad

For some boys, when the sexual abuse started they knew right away that they hated it. It might have hurt physically, and it was scary. When a boy is being abused by someone with a lot of power over him, the abuse can go on for a long time even when he hates it. There are many ways for the abuser to use power to make the abuse continue. Once it has happened, a boy can begin to feel that he kind of agreed to the abuse and has no right to stop it no matter how he feels about it.

Here are some of the ways abusers use power to make the abuse continue.

Physical Power

People with physical power can be really scary. They can threaten to hurt or kill you or the people you love. They can make it look like there is no way to protect yourself or the people you care about from them.

Example

Anthony's mom has had a hard time for a long time. After she'd been drinking, she would get angry at him and his sister. She'd often hit all of them when she was mad. Once she broke his arm when she hit him with a broomstick, and he lied to the doctor about how it happened so his mother wouldn't get in trouble. One night she came to his bed and put her hand on his penis and started to rub it. She said he was "her little man." He could smell the alcohol on her breath. Anthony was afraid to say anything because he knew she'd be furious and really hurt him. And he wasn't sure anyone would believe that he was being sexually molested by his own mother!

Knowledge Power

Someone with this kind of power can manipulate you to cooperate for a long time. Manipulation (*man-IP-you-LAY-shun*) happens when one person uses words or ideas to make another person feel trapped. He feels like he *has* to go along with something. A manipulated person feels like there is no way out and no way to stop what's happening.

Example

Billy never knew his dad. He always wondered what it would be like to have one. When his mom started dating Curtis, he really liked it. They spent more and more time together, and Billy thought that finally he really had a dad. One day, Curtis told Billy that he wanted to "check him out" and see if "things were okay." When Billy let him, Curtis masturbated him until he came. Billy felt awful. He couldn't believe Curtis would do that. Curtis kept asking him to do it again. When Billy said he didn't want to, Curtis got furious. He said he wouldn't come around any more and that Billy's family would be "out on the street." He said Billy was a baby and a "faggot." Billy felt like he had to let Curtis do it again.

Relationship Power

If someone abusive in your life had power because you depended on them or they were older, this was a really tough place to be. Another way people can have power over us is when we want them to like us. It's especially tough if you really liked this person or he or she was really important in your life. This can even happen with kids who are close to your own age if you feel like you have to do something sexual to be a part of the group. For example, to join some gangs, there are sexual "tests" that can be abusive and dangerous.

Examples

Tyrone had moved to a new school. He felt really out of place until Jason invited him to hang out with some of his friends. After Tyrone had hung out with them for a few times, they started to talk more about their gang. He noticed the other kids at school gave him a lot of respect the more he hung out with Jason. One night Jason invited him to "really" join the gang. Tyrone said he wanted to be a part of the gang. Suddenly a bunch of guys grabbed Tyrone and pulled off his pants. They shoved him over the fender of a junk car, yanked his pants down and held him while Jason raped him. Afterward, they congratulated him on being a member of the gang.

James lived in a foster home after his mother died. He went to the foster home when he was 11, and it was okay for the first year. As he grew older, his foster mother began treating him differently. She'd come to his bedroom and kiss him goodnight too long. One day she started rubbing his back in a way that didn't feel right. A month later, after she rubbed his back she put his hand on her breast. James was so embarrassed he didn't know who to tell or what to do. He was sure that he'd be accused of "lying," and that no one would take his word over the foster mom's. He just tried to stay away from her as much as possible.

Survival

Some kids have no one to depend on, even for the basic things in life like food, clothing, and shelter. There are people who use their power to provide these things (or the money to buy them) to manipulate kids into sexual behavior. Many kids who run away from home end up trying to survive by becoming prostitutes or participating in child pornography. Child pornography is when an abuser takes pictures (or uses a video camera) of kids while they are naked and/or performing sexual acts.

Example

Sandy left home when he was thirteen to get away from his dad's hitting him all the time. When he reached the city, he tried to panhandle (asking people for money on the street), but he couldn't get much money. One day a man offered him twenty dollars if Sandy would suck his penis. Sandy did it, and although he felt awful afterwards, he began trading sex for money as a way to live. It seemed the only way to make enough money to survive.

All of these boys in the examples felt bad about the sexual abuse. It was hard for them to get out of it. They felt that they had no way out. The person or people who were abusing them were too powerful in their lives to find a way out.

What to Remember

- **For a lot of reasons, sexual abuse is often hard to stop, even when the boy hates it.**

- **All kids deserve help to stop sexual abuse.**

- **When an abuser uses his or her power to be sexual with a kid, it is unfair and wrong.**

Your Turn

What is hardest about sexual abuse for you? (Check off as many ideas as match the way you feel. Add any thoughts you had that we left out.)

❑ I was afraid of the person(s).

❑ I didn't want people to be mad at me.

❑ I liked the person.

❑ It didn't happen all the time.

❑ I thought I'd go to jail.

❑ I thought she'd go to jail.

❑ I had no choice.

❑ I was afraid it meant I was a faggot.

❑ I felt angry, but didn't want anyone to know.

❑ I felt stuck.

❑ I was afraid I'd be taken out of my home.

❑ I didn't know who to tell.

❑ I didn't think anyone would believe me.

❑ I was afraid my family would lose their home.

❑ I liked other things we did together.

❑ I thought he'd hurt the people I love.

❑ I thought he'd hurt me.

❑ I was afraid I'd go hungry.

❑ I felt used and dirty.

❑ I thought she'd hurt herself.

❑ I didn't want rumors spread around school.

❑ Nothing

_____

_____

_____

_____

As bad as sexual abuse is, somehow you got through it. Write down some of the ways you got through it.

_____

_____

_____

_____

_____

_____

Your Space

Chapter 5

Sorting Out Feelings

When it comes to talking about and sorting out feelings, most boys don't get much practice. It's not that guys don't have feelings. It's that guys are often taught to hold many of their feelings in or to ignore them.

So what happens when a boy has to deal with something like sexual abuse, something that causes feelings that are hard to deal with? Not having much practice at sorting out and talking about feelings can make things especially tough.

One of the problems is that even when you ignore feelings, they don't go away by themselves. You end up with a lot of difficult stuff inside, and no helpful and safe way to get it out. This leaves the door open for feelings to come out in ways that aren't helpful or might be unsafe. A guy may not see how acting in hurtful and unsafe ways connects with being sexually abused.

Knowing More Helps

We get more control over our feelings by talking about them. That's because feelings are like a lot of other things. The more you know about them, the better you can make your choices about how to handle them. More and more men are learning that talking about feelings works.

In Chapter 1, we talked about how the physical injury of a broken arm is like the injuries that can occur to a guy's thoughts and feelings when he is sexually abused. In this chapter, we'll talk about some of these feelings and how they can be affected by sexual abuse. As you read, you might think, "Yeah, I know how that feels," or "No, I never felt like that." That's a great way to start learning about your feelings. Learning about feelings makes them easier to talk about.

Feeling Guilty and Ashamed

Most kids who are sexually abused believe it was somehow their fault or that they deserved it. They may believe they did something to cause the abuse, or that there must have been something about them that made the abuser want to abuse them. When kids believe the abuse was their fault, they end up feeling guilty. Kids also feel ashamed when they believe they are bad or worthless because the abuse happened to them.

Feeling guilt and shame usually doesn't happen to kids by accident. Often the abuser told them that the abuse was their fault or that they deserved it because of something they did or didn't do. What makes things worse is that most abusers *want* kids to feel this way. If the abuser can make the kid believe it was his fault, and not the abuser's, then the kid will be less likely to tell the secret.

Abusers do this by saying things like, "So why were you always hanging around here if you didn't want it to happen?" or "You didn't stop me so you must have wanted it," or "I know you liked it."

Sometimes abusers try to make kids feel guilty in other ways. They may say, "If you tell anyone, I'll have a heart attack," or even "This would kill your mother if she ever found out." Many abusers are experts at making others feel guilty and ashamed. It's their way of making sure you keep their secret. The fact is, nothing you said, did, felt, or thought made you deserve the abuse.

Here's a list of some reasons kids feel guilty. In the "On Second Thought" list, there's a different way to look at the situation.

I feel guilty because . . .	On second thought . . .
I sometimes enjoyed the feelings in my body during the abuse.	Our bodies are built so that they give us good feelings sexually. Sexual feelings are not bad. They are natural. Being curious about sex is also natural. Being forced, tricked, bribed or encouraged to have sex before you want or are ready to is what is confusing and hurtful.
I sometimes felt special and cared for by the person who abused me.	The abuser may have treated you in a special way. Attention, compliments, and gifts are things that can make anyone feel special.
I was doing something I wasn't supposed to do when the abuse happened (went to a party, sneaked out to meet someone, drank beer...)	Even if you were breaking a family rule, it doesn't mean you deserved to be sexually abused. But, it can make it harder to tell. You did not deserve to be abused no matter what else you might have done.
I couldn't stop the abuse.	Most kids can't stop the abuse by themselves, even when they fight back.
I didn't tell.	Most kids don't tell, especially at first. You may have been too afraid, or embarrassed, or you felt too ashamed. You may have worried that others wouldn't believe you. There are lots of reasons that kids don't tell (re-read Chapter 2 for some examples).

Feeling Alone

It's not unusual for a boy to feel more and more alone after the abuse. He may believe he can't get close to anyone because they will find out about the secret, and then think less of him. The boy may blame himself for the abuse and he thinks others will blame him too. Or, the boy may be afraid that getting close to someone else may lead to more abuse. Again, the boy blames himself for the abuse and says to himself, "I made my stepfather want to abuse me, maybe that would happen with my uncle too."

When a kid feels this alone, he might begin to feel like he doesn't fit in anymore. He ends up feeling pretty bad about himself. He spends a lot of time alone because friendships are too hard, too complicated, or too scary because of the abuse. Too often, a loner is picked on by other kids, leading to fights and other trouble. The boy ends up feeling like he has no one on his side and no one he can trust. You don't deserve that. No one does.

Feeling Angry

Most kids have some angry feelings about the abuse. Some kids know who they are angry with and why. They know they are angry at the abuser, or at a family member who doesn't believe them or didn't protect them, or at a friend who told the secret.

At other times, kids are not as clear about why they're angry or who they're angry with. For some guys, feeling and showing anger feels too dangerous. If a boy comes from a family where anger is shown only in hurtful and dangerous ways, he may not know that anger can also be shown in safe and okay ways. Some kids think that anger is the only okay feeling for a boy, so the boy acts angry even when he's feeling something else, like sad or scared.

Angry feelings are not bad feelings. Anger can be helpful. Our anger can be what gives us the courage to say, "It was not my fault!" and "This is not going to ruin my life!"

There are times when angry feelings can get too big to handle. A boy may feel like his anger is controlling him rather than the other way around. If you are doing things that make you feel bad, or sorry, or scared when you're angry, you can change this with help. Many people have learned to have angry feelings and also feel in control of them. You can too.

Feeling Sad

It's not unusual for a boy to feel mixed up about sharing sad feelings with others. He may wonder if other people will see him as less strong if he shows his sad feelings. This leaves a boy torn between needing support and not knowing if it's okay to ask for and get it.

The problem is, if the boy doesn't get the support he needs, he can end up feeling worse than ever. There are times when sad feelings get so deep that they will not go away without the help of a therapist or doctor.

So what's to be sad about? For some boys, it feels like they have lost something important, like a sense of trust, when the abuser was also someone they liked a lot. Other boys might be sad that the abuse ever happened and that they had to live with the secret so long. And then others may be sad because of the way other people acted after finding out about the abuse. These are just a few things about abuse that could trigger your sad feelings.

There are times when a boy just doesn't know that he has sad feelings. Perhaps he had to hide his feelings for so long that they became buried deep down inside. Or, the boy may not have been in a situation where he was safe enough to show some feelings. In that case, the boy did what he needed to do at the time. As he begins to feel safer, he can start to look at feelings he wasn't able to before.

If you've had to bury your sad feelings deep inside for a long time, it can be especially hard and even scary when they start to come out. It may not feel good at the time, but it can be a really good sign. It's a step toward healing the injuries caused by sexual abuse. And talking about it with someone can be a good step toward learning to feel good again.

Feeling Scared

For a lot of guys, the abuse was a frightening experience. The abuser may have physically hurt the boy or threatened to. The abuser may have threatened to hurt or kill someone he cared about if the boy told the secret. A lot of abusers tell kids that all sorts of horrible things will happen if anyone ever finds out.

For other guys, the biggest fear was that someone else would find out about the abuse. They worried about what their families and friends would think. If the abuser was someone the boy cared about, he may have been afraid of what would happen to the abuser if anyone found out. The boy may have also feared that he would be taken out of his home.

Sometimes the person who abuses sexually is abusive in other ways too. Hurting a kid's body on purpose (physical abuse) or constantly hurting a kid's feelings (emotional abuse) are also types of abuse. If you saw someone else be physically, emotionally, or sexually abused, it may have been as scary and painful as your own abuse. For some kids, it feels even worse.

Many kids who've seen others be abused feel guilty or bad that they couldn't stop the abuse. If something like this happened to you, we want to say this loud and clear: It was NOT your fault! Because you were a kid you didn't have as much power as the abuser, and you couldn't protect someone else. It's totally unfair that you had to worry about these things. You deserved and needed the help and protection of an adult, and so did any other children who were abused.

Feeling Confused, Having Mixed Feelings

Feelings usually aren't all one way or the other. People can have lots of different feelings at the same time. Sometimes this can be confusing, especially if those feelings seem like opposites.

For example, what if the abuser was someone you cared about? There may be times when you're so angry that you wish the abuser were dead, or hurt, or that you'd never see him or her again. At other times, you might miss that person and want the old relationship back with or without the sexual part.

It's normal to have mixed or even opposite feelings about some things. It just means that figuring it out takes more time, some thinking, and maybe some help.

Important Ideas

- **Abuse usually hurts a guy's feelings, his pride, and his sense of trust in other people.**

- **Ignored feelings don't go away by themselves, they just come out in other ways.**

- **The more you know about feelings, the better you can make choices about how to handle them.**

- **Talking about injured feelings with someone you trust can help you feel better.**

Your Turn

1. Learning about feelings can make them easier to talk about. Below is a list of feelings you may have had because of the abuse. Put a checkmark by any of the feelings you've had. Write about a time you recently felt this way.

Example

Angry: I feel angry when the abuser says he/she never abused me.

❑ Guilty, Ashamed: _____

_____

❑ Embarrassed: _____

_____

❑ Alone, Lonely: _____

_____

❑ Angry, Mad: _____

_____

❑ Sad, Unhappy: _____

_____

❑ Scared: _____

_____

❑ Confused, Mixed Feelings: _____

_____

❑ Other feelings we haven't listed: _____

_____

2. Which of these feelings is hardest for you to deal with or talk about?

_____

Easiest? _____

Scariest? _____

Which feelings do you think you might need help with?

_____

_____

3. If you had a friend who had been sexually abused, what advice would you give to try and help him/her feel better?

_____

_____

_____

4. Can you apply the advice you'd give to a friend to yourself? Why or why not?

_____

_____

_____

_____

5. You deserve to hear "It was not your fault!" from other people and yourself. Most boys need to hear this message everyday for awhile before they begin to believe it. Plan a way that you can say this to yourself on a daily basis. Sometimes it helps to have a physical activity to go with it. For example, you might try saying this to yourself several times as you jog, exercise, or hit a punching bag. Try saying it to yourself now. How does it feel? A little shaky? Try it again, and this time like you mean it. Now, write down your plan for how you will give yourself this message each day.

_____

_____

_____

Your Space

Chapter 6

Old Coping / New Coping

Sexual abuse causes strong feelings that are difficult to handle alone. But most kids do handle these feelings alone at least some of the time. In this chapter, we will look at some of the ways kids cope with abuse. *Coping* means all the ways people try to help themselves with their feelings or problems so they can go on with their lives.

However you tried to deal with the abuse, you probably did the best job you knew how in a terrible situation. You were in a crisis and you needed emergency help. When the abuse was a secret, you could not get the help and protection you needed. You had to create your own ways to feel better and safer. The ways you figured out to keep your life going during and after the abuse are the ways you were *coping*. Here are some ways kids have made themselves feel a little better for a while:

- eating

- taking a long walk

- throwing things

- being alone in your room

- drinking beer

- playing video games

- reading books

As you take a look at the ways you learned to deal with the abuse, you may decide that some of your old ways of coping aren't helping anymore. Perhaps they even get in the way of what you want for yourself.

Example

Matthew had been molested by his stepfather on and off for two years. His stepdad isn't doing it much lately, because he isn't home most of the time anymore. Before the molesting began, Matthew did okay in school and usually enjoyed the stuff he got to do with his scout troop. He thought maybe he'd like to be an Eagle Scout one day. But now, Matthew doesn't feel like doing much. He sits at home most of the time, and sleeps as much as he can. Sometimes he even sleeps at school, and his grades are dropping. When his mom lectures him, he feels even less like doing or feeling anything and wants to sleep some more. Sometimes he misses his friends in scouts and the fun they used to have, but he says "I'm too tired" when his mom asks him if he wants to go to a meeting.

Matthew is using "not caring" and "sleeping" as a way to cope with the abuse. But now, his way of coping is getting in the way of doing the things he used to enjoy. With help, Matthew can get back to enjoying these things or finding new stuff to do. If changing some of the ways you deal with problems is something you want to do, you can do it. It will take work, and you may need help from others, but it's worth it to get your life back on a track that you choose it to be on.

Coping

It may be helpful to think of ways of coping as tools for dealing with problems and difficult feelings. A beginning carpenter usually doesn't have many tools, maybe just a hammer and a saw. He may not know all the best ways to use the hammer and saw in different situations. Like a beginning carpenter, most kids don't have many tools for dealing with problems and feelings. Have you ever seen a really little kid having a temper tantrum? It was pretty obvious that he was having a hard time dealing with the feelings inside him. He wasn't old enough yet to have collected many tools.

Another way to think about it . . .

Each time a carpenter runs into a new situation, he figures out how to handle it, either by using the tools he's got in new ways, or by getting new tools. The first time he has to bolt something together, he realizes that he needs a wrench. When he puts up a wall, he gets a level and learns how to use it.

Like the carpenter, you collect more tools as you get more experience and run into new situations. Without help in learning how to use new tools, a new carpenter might try to use the hammer on a bolt, or give up and nail the pieces together in the old ways that he's used to, even though it won't last as long or hold as well.

When something like sexual abuse happens to kids, the same kind of thing happens. If the abuse is a secret and the boy can't get the help he needs and deserves, then he has to create emergency coping tools on his own. Below are some of the emergency tools we've seen kids use to cope with sexual abuse.

Separating Yourself from the Abuse

When they're being abused, the feelings kids have hurt a lot. When they can't make the person stop hurting them, they may try to separate themselves from the feelings caused by the hurt.

Alcohol and Drugs

Using alcohol or drugs to numb their feelings is one way that kids separate themselves from the abuse. If you are using alcohol or drugs now or have in the past, it may have been one of the ways you tried to escape hurting. The problem is that using alcohol or drugs to cope leads to more problems — and even more hurting.

A big part of coping better is learning how to deal with difficult feelings head-on instead of numbing them out. Using alcohol or drugs to numb feelings messes up a kid's life and keeps him from learning and practicing better ways of coping.

Another problem is that when people use alcohol or drugs to cope, it's often hard to stop. If you want to stop, but aren't sure you can do it alone, help is available. Talk about it with your counselor or another helpful adult, or look under Alcoholics Anonymous (AA) or Narcotics Anonymous (NA, for help with quitting drugs) in your phone book. These groups have helped many people stop using drugs or alcohol. When you call, they should be able to tell you about meetings in your area. Some meetings are for teens only.

Spacing Out / Forgetting

Sometimes, when something horrible happens, something that is too confusing, too painful, and too hard to handle at the time, a person's mind finds special ways to separate itself from the abuse. One way this can happen is for the person to forget the horrible thing and not remember it for some time. Other people may remember what happened, but to the person it seems like a dream or like it happened to someone else.

Many people have said that while the abuse was happening, it all felt unreal. Some have said that it felt like they actually left their bodies while the abuse was happening. When an abused person experiences this he may be afraid to tell anyone because he is afraid it might sound too weird. It's not. It's just a very special emergency tool that some people use in horrible situations. Counselors and therapists call this dissociation (*diss-so-see-AY-shun*).

"Forgetting" and "dreaming" helped the person deal with a horrible situation. The problem is that this way of coping can become automatic. A kid may start to use it more and more in situations that aren't emergencies. Then he may find that he has a hard time concentrating in school or other parts of his life where he wants to concentrate. The boy may begin to feel numb all the time. When you're numb, you can't feel the good stuff in your life or protect yourself well from the stuff you need to notice. A therapist or counselor can help you change this if it has become a problem for you, and we'll talk more about it later on.

Another way to think about it . . .

This way of coping doesn't only get used after sexual abuse. People have coped with lots of different situations that were way too hard by spacing out and forgetting. Sometimes this kind of spacing out or forgetting comes along with nightmares and strong images that are like reliving the bad situation (flashbacks).

Then it is called Post Traumatic Stress Disorder (PTSD). Counselors began to see this a lot when soldiers came back from fighting in the Vietnam war. One therapist who works with abused kids wrote that kids with PTSD are dealing with "Pretty Tough Stuff, Dude!"*

Just Not Caring

Another way that a boy can separate from the abuse is to convince himself that it was "no big deal." He remembers what happens, but keeps telling himself it just didn't matter. This is sometimes called "minimizing" (*MIN-ih-MY-zing*) or being "in denial." The problem with this way of coping is that the boy can start to feel like that about everything — his friends, family, school and himself. The boy ends up not enjoying, or caring about, or feeling anything. When a kid gives up feeling and caring, he also gives up on the good things in life too. You don't deserve that!!

Putting Anger in the Wrong Place

As you've read before, most kids have angry feelings about the abuse. When it's not safe to be angry at the person who abused you, sometimes the angry feelings come out sideways, in places and at people where they don't belong.

---

*Cunningham, C., & MacFarlane, K. (1996). *When Children Abuse: Group Treatment Strategies for Children with Impulse Control Problems*, p. 165. Brandon, VT: Safer Society Press.

Taking Anger Out On Yourself

Kids often believe that when bad things happen to them, it must be because they deserve it. If you felt this way, you probably ended up feeling pretty bad about yourself, and you may be doing things to hurt yourself because of feeling so bad. We hope that at this point you are working hard at knowing that you don't deserve that anger. One big part of getting your life back on track is feeling safe enough to put anger where it belongs. It's important to learn a way of dealing with anger that doesn't end up causing more problems for you.

You have a right to be angry at the abuser. You have a right to be angry that this happened to you. You have a right to be angry at the people who couldn't or wouldn't protect you. And, it's okay to be angry — even furious — at people you also care about.

Taking It Out On Others

Sometimes, when a boy is unable to deal with his angry feelings about the abuse or the abuser, his anger begins to pour into other areas of his life and at other people. Some guys take their anger out on others by bullying, hitting, calling names, yelling, blaming other people for any little thing that doesn't go their way, and so on. Perhaps the boy can't express angry feelings at the abuser because he is afraid the abuser may hurt him. Or if the abuser is someone who is important to the boy he may be afraid that expressing anger will make the abuser stop caring about him.

Even though the boy can't express his anger at the person he's angry with, the anger is still there. The boy may begin doing things that are hurtful to others as a way to get rid of the anger. Hurting others won't really help the boy feel better. It only leads to more and more problems for the boy.

Some kids who have been sexually abused deal with their feelings by sexually touching other kids. For example, some kids use sexual touching because the person who abused them taught them that's the way to express caring feelings. For others, sexually touching a littler kid or someone who doesn't want or understand it is how they express their anger. It can be a boy's way of saying, "Someone hurt me, so I'll hurt someone else." The boy uses sexual touching to feel more powerful and in control again.

This kind of sexual touching leads to many problems. The boy ends up feeling bad about what he's doing, and he still doesn't feel in control of himself or his life. That's because he hasn't dealt with his own abuse, the thing that made him feel bad and out of control in the first place. And now, the kids the boy was sexually touching also end up hurt and confused. No one deserves that, not you, and not anyone else.

If you are doing this kind of touching, you need to stop. Some kids find they can't stop on their own. They need help to learn to stop. If you have learned to express your feelings with unwanted sexual touching, you need and deserve help to learn to deal with your feelings in a way that doesn't hurt you or anyone else.

Sexual feelings and being curious about sex are things that are normal and good. Encouraging, bribing, tricking, or forcing someone into sexual touching is not good for anyone. If you are worried about any sexual touching you have done in the past, please talk about it with a counselor or therapist, or find someone else who can help. You probably have questions about what will happen if you tell a therapist about any unwanted sexual touching you have done with others in the past. Perhaps it will help to show the therapist this part of the book. Ask him or her to talk to you about what usually happens when a kid tells about sexually touching another kid who didn't want it or understand it.

Some good questions to ask a therapist may be: (1) Do you have to report this to anyone else? (2) If you do, what happens then? (3) Will you be there to help me straighten all this out?

The answers to these questions will depend on several things. You and your therapist will figure this out together. The main goal is to get the unwanted sexual touching to stop. That's what's best for everybody.

What Do I Do Now?

If you have taken your anger out on yourself or others, you can change if you want to. But in most cases it will take the help of a counselor or therapist, plus your own hard work.

There are many other warning signs that can let you know that your problems have gotten too big to handle alone. Here's a list of some of them.

Warning Signs

Put a √ or an X in the box next to questions that you would answer with a "yes." Since being abused . . .

❑ Have you thought about hurting yourself or have you hurt yourself on purpose (for example, by cutting or burning yourself)?

❑ Have you thought about suicide?

❑ Do you often put yourself in dangerous situations (such as by driving too fast, driving drunk or drugged, letting yourself ride with other people who drive too fast or are drunk or drugged)?

❑ Have you run away from home? Do you think about doing it?

❑ Have you been sexually active without knowing if you really want to be? Do you feel like you have no control over being sexual or not?

❑ Have you ever felt like touching or have you touched someone else's body sexually who didn't want you to? Have you sexually touched someone who was too young, too drunk, or mentally disabled to understand or to say no?

❑ Do you think about having sex with little kids or against someone else's will?

❑ Are you using alcohol or drugs?

❑ Have you stolen or shoplifted anything recently?

❑ Have you begun to smoke or increase your smoking?

❑ Do you wish you were never born? Do you think other people feel this way about you?

❑ Do you feel like nobody cares about you? Do you feel like you don't deserve to be cared about?

❑ Do you feel tired all the time? Do you want to just sleep a lot?

❑ Do you feel like you always have too much energy and can't concentrate or relax?

❑ Do you cry often, even when you're not sure what's wrong? Do you feel like you want to cry, but don't let yourself?

❑ Do you often get angry over little things that didn't bother you in the past?

❑ Do any of your fantasies during masturbation bother you later?

❑ Do you masturbate when you're angry?

❑ When you feel bad do you do things that might get you into trouble if other people knew?

❑ Do you rub or touch your private parts (masturbate) in public (such as in school, in church, or in other public places) where people notice it and get upset with you?

❑ When you are angry or feeling bad, are you doing things that hurt other people? Are you afraid that you might?

❑ Are you getting into a lot of fights with other people? Damaging property?

❑ Are you unable to concentrate at school or on your homework? Have your grades gone down?

❑ Do you have trouble sleeping? Have frequent nightmares?

❑ Have you gained or lost a lot of weight without trying?

❑ Do you feel like eating all the time? Are you overeating and feeling bad about it? Do you ever make yourself throw up?

Getting Help

If you've answered yes to any of these questions, remember that lots of other kids have had the same problems. It's important that you tell someone who can and will help. If you don't know anyone who can and will help, look back to the end of Chapter 1, at the section on "Some Ways to Find Help." Don't give up!

Important Ideas

- Emergency situations call for emergency coping.

- You did the best job you knew how in your emergency situation.

- Some ways of coping and some feelings about the abuse can spill over into hurting yourself and other people.

- If your old ways of coping aren't working well for you anymore, you can change them!

- Changing them will take time, attention, work, and help from other people.

Your Turn

Write about some of the emergency tools you used to help you cope with sexual abuse. Do you use them now? What is happening when you use them now?

_____

_____

_____

_____

_____

_____

Do your emergency tools still help you cope? Do they ever get in the way of what you want for yourself? How? Are there things about how you deal with your life that you want to change? Which ones?

_____

_____

_____

_____

_____

_____

_____

Think of steps you can take to start making these changes. Try asking someone you trust for suggestions too. Write down the ways you think of or the suggestions you get. After you write down these ideas, try making a plan for how you could make each idea work for you. Start with the thing you want to have happen at the end (the result), then work backwards.

_____

_____

_____

_____

_____

Your Space

Chapter 7

Choosing Your Track

Sexual abuse usually causes a crisis or emergency situation in a person's life. Dealing with the abuse and the fact that it was a secret takes up a lot of energy that he could have used for other things. It usually affects how a boy thinks and feels about himself and about his relationships with others. In this chapter, we'll look at some of the ways this happens. We'll also look at how you can begin to make your own choices about how you want to think, feel and live.

How Abuse Lowers Self-Esteem

Esteem is the positive way you feel about someone you admire. Self-esteem is the deep down feeling that you really are an okay person. Most people start out life with that okay feeling of self-esteem. But you can lose self-esteem when bad things happen, especially when someone you care about, someone you thought cared about you, hurts you on purpose.

Some kids who are sexually abused also have to deal with other hurtful things in their lives. Another way a person's self-esteem can be injured is by being physically hurt on purpose (being hit, kicked, thrown against a wall, or hurt by a weapon), especially by someone who is supposed to care. This is physical abuse. Still another way self-esteem can be injured is when a parent or other important people call a person names a lot of the time, such as telling him he's worthless or stupid or lazy or ugly. This is emotional abuse.

When bad things happen to kids, they often feel like they must have deserved it, that is, unless there's someone around to show them the truth. When kids have to cope alone, they find ways to try to explain this bad experience to themselves. According to some kids we've talked to, their thoughts sound something like this:

"She hit me because I'm bad."

or

"He molested me because he thought I wanted it."

or

"They hate me because I'm stupid."

When you believe the abuse was your fault, the negative thoughts and feelings you have about the abuse get connected to your thoughts and feelings about yourself. There are a lot of negative messages that you may tell yourself to try to make some sense of the abuse. This is called "negative self-talk." It's another way a person tries to cope with what's happening to him. Unfortunately, you may hear these types of messages from other people too, like family members, on T.V., or from kids at school. They may not even be talking about you or your situation, but the messages are still there.

A father says, "I'll beat some sense into you."

or

**A stepmom says,
"You could do it if you weren't so stupid and clumsy."**

or

**A person on a talk show says,
"Look at that faggot, he deserved to be raped."**

When you hear these kinds of messages enough, it's likely that you'll begin to believe them, even though they are not really true. Then you may begin to say these things to yourself, too.

Steps to Getting Back on Your Track

If your self-esteem has been injured because of abuse, we'd like to say something again loud and clear: You Don't Deserve It! The truth is, no one deserves it. Fortunately, you can change your self-esteem if you want to just as other kids have — you're not stuck with what the abuse or the abuser handed you. Where do you begin? You already have begun by reading and working through this book. It's important that the negative thoughts and feelings you now have about yourself be reconnected with what caused them in the first place — the abuse. Then you can begin to work on connecting more positive thoughts and feelings with what they should be connected with — *you.*

Changing Self-Talk

Self-talk is what you say to yourself inside your mind about yourself, other people, and the world. It can be positive or negative. One big step to feeling better inside is changing negative self-talk back into positive self-talk. We know this is not a simple step, especially if you've been thinking negative messages for a long time. You may not even realize you're doing it. It will take some real effort to figure out what messages you've been giving yourself.

To change negative self-talk into positive self-talk, first start listening to your thoughts. Some messages are connected with the abuse ("It's my fault," or "I deserved it."). But negative self-talk usually begins to creep into other areas of your life, too. When you're meeting someone new, you might hear yourself thinking, "I know he won't like me." Or when you think about trying something new, you might catch yourself thinking, "I could never do that." If your self-talk sounds like these messages, you're talking yourself out of doing a lot of fun stuff and avoiding knowing a lot of people.

Catching that Thought

The first step in changing negative self-talk is to catch yourself doing it. Usually these thoughts just float by in the back of your mind without your noticing. You may feel the bad feelings that go with them, but you don't realize that there are words that started the feelings.

One way to catch that thought is to keep a piece of paper in your pocket. Make a mark on the paper every time you hear yourself thinking something negative or bad about yourself. The next step is to write down the negative thought as soon as you realize you're thinking about it.

Replacing the Message

Replacing the message means thinking of new positive things to say to yourself. Sometimes people start by thinking of words that are the opposite of the negative thoughts they've been having.

Changing Self-Talk

Step 1: Catching that thought	Step 2: Replacing the message
a. Notice what you're feeling, especially when you feel bad.	a. Think of something positive about yourself.
b. Notice what you're thinking when those bad feelings happen.	b. Write that thought down.
c. Count how many negative thoughts you have about yourself in a day.	c. Keep a copy of your positive thought somewhere you can see it often.
d. Write down your thoughts.	d. Each time you hear yourself thinking a negative thought, think "STOP!" and then say your positive thought to yourself.
Example: *"Nobody will ever like me."*	Example: *"STOP! Buddy and Frank are my friends, so other guys will like me too."*

Step 3: Practice!

Example

Tyler began counting his negative self-talk thoughts and was shocked to find out that on Thursday he had 13 by the end of the day! When he wrote them down, he saw they were all familiar, even though he hadn't realized before that they came so often. He had been thinking about asking a girl out, but every time he thought about it he found himself saying things like "God, she probably doesn't even know who I am or if she does, she thinks I'm an idiot." He also realized he was cutting himself down about other friendships. When a boy in his history class told him to stop by at a party he was having, Tyler found himself thinking, "Why would he want a dweeb like me at the party?" After a week of keeping track of his negative thoughts, he was ready for the next step: replacing them!

Tyler knew he really wanted to go to that party. Even though he felt a little weird about it at first, he began practicing saying positive things to himself about going to the party. One message he used to replace the negative messages was, "Some of the guys think I'm pretty funny. We have a good time hanging out. I'd invite someone like me to a party." Tyler noticed that after awhile he didn't feel so weird about the positive self-messages. He also found that he was feeling more like he might actually go to the party.

Think about some encouraging words that you can say to yourself the next time your negative self-talk comes up. Think of what you might say to a good friend in the same situation, and then be a good friend to yourself. You don't deserve anything mean from yourself or from anyone else. What's your new message? Try saying it out loud. Write it down. Put it on a little sticky note or a piece of paper and tape it inside your wallet or in a notebook where you'll see it every day. Think about how it feels. Talk to someone else about it if you want to.

Practice!

For most kids, the new messages take time to sink in. It takes practice. Make a plan for when you'll practice it, and then do it several times a day. It may feel awkward or silly at first, but positive self-talk has helped many kids (and adults, too!).

It's important that you hear positive messages from yourself *and* from others. If you're not hearing positive messages from others, go back over the steps we listed in Chapter 1 for getting more support in your life.

Putting Words Into Action

While replacing negative messages with positive ones is a good step, it only works in the long run if your actions fit your words. You won't feel better about yourself if you often do things that make you feel guilty, ashamed, angry, or sad. A lot of kids need to work on not feeling guilty for the things they're not responsible for — like the abuse, for example, or a divorce. But at the same time, feeling guilty, ashamed, angry, and sad is a normal response when kids knowingly do things that hurt themselves or others — like lying, using drugs, drinking, shoplifting, or having unprotected sex with partners they don't really care about, for example. These feelings give you the message that something is not right, something needs to change. No one can really feel good about himself until he takes responsibility for his own actions. And remember, you are not responsible for anyone's actions but your own.

Be Willing to Try

All of us have things we are good at. Find yours. We all have certain strengths, talents, and gifts to share. But you can only know what it feels like to be good at something if you try. It's even okay to try and then find out that you're not good at something or to try something new and let yourself not be good in the beginning until you learn how. It helps you learn more about you, and you can be proud of yourself for trying. The world needs your gifts, and you need to share what's inside you. You can practice being willing to try by trying out positive self-talk.

Sexuality

Another area that all people want to feel okay about themselves is in their sexuality. But just like many other areas in a kid's life, sexual abuse can make dealing with sexuality more confusing and more difficult.

The words "sexual" and "abuse" don't belong together. Human beings are naturally interested in sexuality. Every person has sexual feelings, thoughts, and experiences, and it can be a good part of life. When some people abuse others, they are using their power to take advantage. Good sex is not about power. It's about being old enough and mature enough to share warm, wonderful, exciting feelings with someone you care about and who cares about you.

In a relationship like this, neither partner uses power over the other to get what he or she wants. Both people have a say, and both people's say counts. No one has the right to force, convince, bribe, or push you into being sexual when you're not sure or don't want to. And you never have the right to force, convince, bribe, or push anyone else sexually. Good sexual relationships can't happen this way. They happen when both partners feel okay about themselves and each other.

Disconnecting Sexuality from Abuse

Because you were abused in a sexual way, sometimes your normal sexual feelings may remind you of the abuse. When this happens, your normal sexual feelings become connected with uncomfortable feelings. For example, some of the things you fantasize about or feel sexual about may worry you.

If your sexual feelings are connected with thoughts and feelings that scare you, worry you, or make you feel guilty or angry, then you are being robbed of some of the positive feelings that sexuality should bring you. It's important that you find a way to *disconnect* the feelings of being sexual and the feelings of being abused. The scary, guilty, worried, angry feelings are connected with abuse, not good sexuality.

Remember that good sexual feelings leave you feeling okay about yourself. If this is not happening for you when you're feeling sexual about another person or fantasizing about sexual things, you should talk with a therapist about it. Too embarrassed? Remember, a therapist won't be surprised or shocked. That's what they're there for — to talk about really difficult stuff and to help you figure it all out.

Many kids wonder if masturbation (giving yourself sexual pleasure) is a normal part of sexuality. The answer is yes. For most kids masturbation is a natural part of learning about and enjoying their own sexuality, especially if they're not spending too much time feeling guilty or worried about it.

If your fantasies during masturbation are connected to the abuse or make you feel scared, worried, guilty, or angry, then it's a sign that sexuality and abuse are still connected. You'll need help getting them unconnected. Again, the best thing to do is talk to a therapist about it. Show them this section if that will help.

Fears About Homosexuality

Many boys worry a lot about what it means if the person who abused them was a man or another boy. They wonder if this means they are gay or homosexual (someone who is more attracted to the same sex). The answer is no. Being abused by someone of the same sex does not make a person homosexual. Sexual orientation — who we are attracted to — is something we discover, not the result of what is done to us.

But what if the boy sometimes enjoyed the sex, or sometimes has sexual fantasies about what happened? Again, our bodies are made so that they give us good feelings sexually. It does not mean that the boy is homosexual.

Boys who were sexually abused are just like boys who have never been sexually abused. Some (a larger percentage) grow up to be heterosexual, attracted more to women. Some (maybe 10 percent) grow up to be homosexual, attracted more to other men. Some (we don't know how many) grow up to be attracted to both women and men (bisexual). Many researchers and scientists think we are born with our sexual orientation — whether we are straight (heterosexual), gay (homosexual), or bisexual.

What if a boy was already having homosexual feelings? Does that mean he deserved the abuse?

No! Being homosexual doesn't make somebody deserve to be sexually abused. Abuse is mostly about power, and sex is used as a weapon. No one should be sexually abused, and people are not more or less valuable because of being attracted more to one sex than the other. Every person is valuable. People who think gays and lesbians deserve to be badly treated are usually afraid of others who are different from them. Your sexual feelings are yours to explore, and no one should take advantage of them to abuse you.

A lot of kids who grow up wondering if they are homosexual feel a great deal of shame, guilt and loneliness because our society still doesn't talk openly about these things. A good therapist or counselor should be able to help a kid sort these feelings out.

What if the abuser was a woman and the boy didn't like it?

Some boys worry that something is wrong with them if the abuser was a woman and they did not enjoy it or feel good about it later. Aren't boys always supposed to enjoy sex? Not really, though this is part of the mixed messages that our society often gives boys about sex. Remember that good sex is never about one person having more power over the other in a sexual way. It's normal to not enjoy it when you felt forced or encouraged into something you didn't choose or feel ready for.

Is it still abuse if the boy enjoyed the sexual part of it?

Yes. Adults should not be involved sexually with children. Women or men who are have been sexually involved with a kid have used their power in unhealthy ways. If the person who abused you was an older kid, or someone about your age who used some threat or bribe, the same unhealthy power issues are involved and become confused with the good sexual feelings. It's just not the best way to learn about sex. It can affect your emotions, your sexual feelings, and your ability to have normal relationships in the future.

Feeling Worried About My Body

Being sexually abused can lead to questions and worries about your body. It's possible that you have had questions like, "Has the abuse permanently hurt my body in any way?" or "Could I have gotten a sexually transmitted disease?" or "Will my body grow up normally?"

The best person to answer these questions is a medical doctor. Being examined by a doctor and talking with him or her about your concerns will help you feel better about what's going on with your body. It may help to remember that doctors are used to talking to people about personal stuff, and none of your questions are weird or unimportant. And yes, the doctor has probably heard something like it before. It may also help to write down your questions in case you forget or get nervous. Take the list of questions with you. If all else fails, you can always just hand the list to the doctor. Medical doctors are supposed to keep your medical records private. There are exceptions, like getting permission from your parents for medical treatments, or reporting physical or sexual abuse. But you can always ask for your questions to be kept private.

Also, don't forget to talk to your doctor about how to have safe sex in the future. Remember that when you make the choice to be sexually active, using a condom is your best protection against getting sexually transmitted diseases. You should also talk to your doctor about how to prevent unwanted pregnancy. It's all a part of being sexually responsible and respecting both yourself and your partner.

Making Choices

Feeling good about yourself involves many things, including your self-esteem, your relationships, your sexuality, and the choices you make in life. If sexual abuse has knocked you off track for awhile, remember you have every right in the world to get back on a track that *you choose*.

Important Ideas

- Most kids who were abused think bad things about themselves — their self-esteem was injured by the abuse and they learn negative self-talk.

- You can help yourself feel better inside by replacing negative self-talk with more positive messages.

- Most people need help to disconnect their sexual feelings from the abuse.

- You deserve to feel good about yourself.

Your Turn

In lots of kids' negative self-talk they call themselves names.

Example

Randy wanted to be a great soccer player, and he made the team. But every time he missed a kick, he'd say to himself, "You stupid spaz!"

Name calling is another kind of negative self-talk that does not help you do better. It just makes you feel worse. Randy could help himself improve his game if he practiced thinking, "How can I do it better?" He can watch other players and learn how they pass, dribble, and head the ball. If nothing went wrong and the ball just didn't go in because someone blocked it, he could think "Good try!" and then work on some new moves to get around the defender.

Do you yell at yourself inside? What kinds of things do you say? Check the box beside any of the statements you say to yourself. If there are other things you say to yourself, write them in.

❏ I'm stupid.   ❏ I suck.

❏ I hate myself.   ❏ I'm not worth crap.

_____

_____

_____

_____

_____

It's easy to get in the habit of yelling at yourself — kids get yelled at by other people a lot. But it can really help to get in the habit of encouraging yourself. When teams get together in a huddle before the game you know they are saying encouraging things! What kinds of encouraging things can you say inside? Write them down.

Examples

Nice try.	It's okay.	I did great.
I can do it.	Good job.	Way to go!
Better next time.	I'm learning!	Great move!

_____

_____

_____

_____

When do you feel best about yourself? Write about a time you felt proud of yourself.

_____

_____

_____

_____

Name three things you are good at.

_____

_____

_____

_____

What are some things you have never tried to do but would like to?

_____

_____

_____

_____

_____

_____

Have you ever tried something that you were not good at, but you felt like you learned something? What was it and what did you learn?

_____

_____

_____

_____

_____

_____

Your Space

Chapter 8

Therapy

Therapy is a strange idea for a lot of people. You or your family may think that therapy is for "crazy" people, so if you go to a therapist you must be kind of crazy. This isn't true. The truth is that a therapist is a person who knows a lot about helping. If you are seeing a therapist, their job is to help you.

I Don't Need Any Help!

We're glad that some things in your life are fine. Therapy won't take away the good stuff. Therapy helps your life get better. Go back to the "warning signs" list in Chapter 6. If you checked a few of the things on that list, chances are you should be in therapy, because a therapist can help with those kinds of problems. That's the part of your life that doesn't have to stay the same. That's the part of your life that could be a lot better.

I'll Figure It Out Myself!

Sometimes it's very hard for a person to figure out his problems. It's like if you were on a train going from California to New York. If somewhere in Kansas a track got switched, you wouldn't know it for a long time. You might get clues, like seeing a palm tree instead of the Empire State Building, but it would take a while. This is the same idea. Maybe anger got off track for you, maybe something else. Therapists are trained to look at the big picture and then help people get their lives back on track.

I Don't Want to Talk About It

Like we said before, guys tend not to want to talk about most feelings. They tend to REALLY not want to talk about sexual abuse. Even adult men say that it's really hard to talk about it. However, they also say that if they'd been able to figure sexual abuse out as kids, parts of their lives might have been less confusing, lonely, and painful.

Therapists are really good with ideas and understanding about sexual abuse. They aren't embarrassed, surprised or shocked. You may be really surprised that having time to talk and getting ideas from a therapist can feel really good.

What Therapy Should Be Like

Therapy and your therapist should feel safe and helpful. Safe means you can say anything or feel anything and your therapist can handle it. Helpful means that your therapist will have lots of ideas on how you can make things better in your life. Therapy will probably be fun sometimes and make you mad or sad other times. That's okay. You can be mad at your therapist and he or she will still like you. Therapists understand that you have lots of different feelings.

Because sexual abuse is usually hard at least in some ways, some of therapy will be hard. But therapists know a lot about balance. Balance here means that for hard parts of the therapy, there will be parts that are about you feeling good about yourself, too.

What Will I Do In Therapy?

Therapy happens lots of ways. When you first meet your therapist, you'll figure out what's going well and feels good in your life. That's so you can make that stuff be a bigger part of your life. You'll also figure out what isn't working so well. That stuff will get attention too. Some therapy is talk, some is play, some may be art, and some therapy is action.

Lots of boys who are molested are sure that they are the only ones ever molested. It can be a relief to meet a therapist who can tell you from experience that you are not the only one. Sometimes a therapist suggests that a boy join a therapy group with other guys who have been molested. Whether you decide to go to a group is up to you, but it often helps to meet at least one other boy who was molested. If you get to meet other guys who were molested, you'll probably find out that: 1) they are normal just like you; 2) sexual abuse confused them a lot (maybe like you); 3) they tried to handle it in ways kind of like you did; and 4) they are learning to make changes in their lives (maybe like you).

What Will My Therapist Tell Other People About Me?

Your therapist should make therapy safe for your ideas and feelings. Most of what you do and say in therapy is confidential (*con-fih-DEN-shul*). Keeping things confidential is different from keeping secrets. The abuser wanted you to keep the sexual things he or she did to you a secret so he or she wouldn't get caught. The secret was to protect the abuser. Confidentiality in therapy should be there to protect *you* and keep you safe.

There are some exceptions to confidentiality, some things that your therapist *must* tell others about. Your therapist may need to tell your family some things in order to keep you safe. And sometimes your family might actually be involved in your therapy. Your therapist will not protect the person or people who molested you. Information about abusers needs to be told so they can't hurt you or others any more. Also, if you are into activities that are dangerous to you or physically threatening to other people, your therapist will probably let important people in your life know. If you have any questions about privacy and therapy, be sure to ask. Say to your therapist, "What kind of things will you tell other people about what I say and feel, and who will you tell?" See what they say.

Ways to Help Your Therapist

People handle sexual abuse lots of ways. When the way they handle it is to keep it very secret, it is harder for a therapist to help. One way to help your therapist help you is to be really honest about what's going on in your life.

Examples

Alonzo had been in therapy for about a year and his life was going pretty well. He was getting along better with his mother and his teachers weren't on his back any more. He was still kind of embarrassed about being in therapy, so he was glad that they were talking about ending. But deep inside something about being molested by his aunt kept bothering him. He just couldn't make it sit right, and he couldn't figure it out on his own. Somewhere inside himself, he kept thinking, "If I was a real man, I should have liked it." That thought kept bugging him, so he finally told his therapist.

Omar was in therapy after his dad molested him. One way Omar made some money was to babysit the neighbors' kids. Four-year-old John would get on Omar's lap while watching T.V. Lately Omar would get an erection when John was sitting on his lap. He even started to think about the boy when he masturbated. When his therapist asked about his sexual fantasies one day, Omar decided to tell him about John.

Another thing to talk about in therapy is if you are dealing with sexual abuse by dissociation. Dissociation is kind of like "spacing out." It's a way of separating yourself or your feelings from awful things that are going on. Dissociation can happen lots of different ways. Here are some examples. Have you had any experiences like these?

You don't remember exactly what happened.

Joseph knows that when he was in Boy Scouts the scout master touched his backside and penis. But when his mom and dad ask, "What did you do," he can't remember. Even when he tries to remember what happened next, he can't.

You know it happened, but you don't feel anything.

Bobby remembers running home after the teenage boys grabbed him and pulled him into the woods. He remembers everything they said and did. But he has no idea how to answer when people ask him "How do you feel?" or "What was it like?" When he thinks about it, he feels numb. It's a really weird feeling — kind of like "no one's home." Even his body feels numb when he thinks about it

You have almost no memory of anything.

Karl's whole family went to court with him when he was ten. He had to testify about his older cousin Karen who molested him. But now that he's thirteen, he has no memory at all of the abuse and even the court part is fuzzy. He doesn't remember testifying. When other people talk about it, he feels weird. His brain gets a strange feeling, but he has no memory.

All these examples are some of the ways dissociation works. It can also happen in other ways. Dissociation is a way to build walls around abuse. Walls at people's houses can be different: some are made of wood, some of brick. Some walls, like in an attic or between the kitchen and dining room, might be only three feet high. Others run right to the ceiling. Some are even made of glass. Just like walls at people's houses, walls around abuse differ from one person to another. Each person who dissociates experiences it in a slightly different way.

The problem with dissociation is that it helps very well while the abuse is happening by keeping you from freaking out. But it is not a good permanent way to help inside. Ideas that are hidden behind walls through dissociation have a way of "leaking out." It's confusing to feel things that just don't make sense logically. For example, if the person who sexually abused you wore a green shirt and you dissociated everything about the abuse, you still might feel weird whenever you see somebody wearing a green shirt.

So let's go back to the idea of how to help your therapist. Tell her or him about any confusing ideas, feelings and experiences. A therapist is like a good detective, and together you can make sense out of things that at first make no sense at all. Once you connect the *real* reason you can't remember or are scared or confused or numb, you're a lot less likely to have these strange feelings. Most things you experience that are connected to the abuse can make sense eventually. A therapist is a good person to help you figure things out.

What If I Hate It?

If you hate therapy, that's a really important thing to notice. Try to figure out why. Maybe you hate the questions your therapist asks. Since therapy is a good place to talk about feelings, it's great to tell your therapist! You could even show him or her this part of the book. You could just say "I hate your questions!" You and your therapist can figure out what can make it easier. Maybe the questions are confusing. Maybe you just don't know the answers and don't want to keep saying that. Maybe you just don't want to talk about it. (Maybe you could YELL about it!)

If you can't work out a way to make therapy helpful for you with this therapist, you may need to try working with a new therapist. Maybe your therapist doesn't know how to help you balance the hard stuff and easy stuff. Sometimes a kid may feel more comfortable with a woman therapist instead of a man, or a man therapist instead of a woman. The idea here is that you and your therapist need to figure out how to make therapy help YOU. It's YOUR time.

Maybe you hate therapy because of outside reasons. Some kids get the message that therapy is a bad thing or that therapy means you are crazy. Family members or other people may say it's too expensive or that it's hard to get you there. Someone may say that "you should be over this."

If people are saying stuff like this, again, talk to your therapist. Then they'll understand and may be able to help the other people understand also.

Remember, it's the therapist's job to help. Therapists can't fix everything. They can't make abuse go away or make feelings stop. They can make things easier to deal with, and most therapists are really good at that.

It doesn't happen very often, but sometimes a therapist might misuse his or her power to involve a person in sexual touching either during sessions or somewhere else. Any therapist who hits you or touches you sexually is being abusive. If this happens to you, tell your parents, your social worker, or a guidance counselor right away, and don't keep seeing this therapist. It is never okay for sexual touching to happen in therapy.

We wish we could say that therapy is really easy and always works quickly. That's not true. Therapy is not like magic and even with a really great therapist, therapy takes work. But over time therapy can help make your life a lot easier and get you back on track a lot faster.

What's Important Here?

- All of us have behavior, ideas and feelings that bother us sometimes.

- Everyone needs help in dealing with confusing feelings about big issues like sexual abuse.

- Therapy is one of the best ways to get help in figuring out your feelings and thoughts about the abuse.

- The best way to help your therapist is to tell the truth, even when you're scared.

- Your therapist has heard about stuff like this from other kids before. You probably won't shock them and they won't think you are weird.

- With a little help, you can feel better, understand more, and make your own choices about your life.

Your Turn

If you are in therapy, what's the best thing about it for you? Check all of the statements that match your experience, or add your own.

❑ My therapist understands what I've gone through.

❑ My therapist has good ideas.

❑ My therapist listens to me.

❑ My therapist has helped some things get easier.

_____

_____

_____

_____

Are there things you wished were different about therapy? Write them down.

_____

_____

_____

_____

_____

_____

_____

If you are not in therapy, list at least one person you might be able to talk to about what has happened in your life that's been hard. Think about who else you might talk to as a backup if the first person wasn't home. Write their names down.

_____

_____

_____

_____

_____

_____

Write any ideas you have about how you can start to talk to one of these people about sexual abuse.

Example

"We had this movie in school about sexual abuse. Well, I could have been in that movie. Can I talk to you about it?"

_____

_____

_____

_____

_____

_____

_____

_____

_____

Your Space

Chapter 9

Now and Later

Y ou may have some questions about how sexual abuse will affect different parts of your life. In this chapter, we'll look at some of the things you may be dealing with because of the abuse. We'll also look at what it might mean to you tomorrow, next year, and later on in your life.

Your Family

Sexual abuse always leads to a family crisis. In a crisis, there are always difficult feelings to cope with. Some families are able to be clear about who they are angry with — the abuser. Often, those families are able to deal with the crisis in a way that eventually helps each family member cope with what has happened. Many of these families found that counseling helped them along. Family counseling has helped many families find new ways to talk about and face problems.

Unfortunately, some families are not able to cope well with this crisis. They may try to keep the abuse a secret, tell the boy to just forget it, or even blame the boy or say he's lying. Nothing gets solved, and there's usually more hurting for the boy and his family.

When Your Family Won't or Can't Help

If your family won't or can't help, you can still get help for yourself. If the abuser was a family member, there are laws that require the family to get help. At times, family members are so much in denial that they refuse to let anyone help at all. They may be unable to keep their children safe. Sometimes, in these cases, the kids have to go live with another family (either with relatives or with a foster family) that is safer. Sometimes this is a temporary solution, and the kids go back home as the adults begin to solve their problems.

In some families, the adults are unable or unwilling to do the work they need to do to solve the problems that are making things unsafe at home. Sometimes, this means the kids can't go back to live with this family, but must stay in their new home with a relative or foster family. Though it is hard not to be able to live with their original family, some kids are able to find a better life in the new family.

When a family splits up, like when parents separate or the kids go to a foster family, kids often feel that it is somehow their fault. If this has happened to you, you need to hear this loud and clear: *Kids can't solve adults' problems*. It's the job of adults to work out their own problems. Sometimes they can't, or won't, or don't do the work. It's hard on the kids when they don't, but it's not the kids' fault. All kids need and deserve the help of grown-ups, including you.

Social Services

The law says that if you are under age 18 and you have been sexually abused, you must be referred to an agency that works to protect children and teens. If you are involved with an agency like this, you probably have a social worker or caseworker. This person may have a lot to do with your life. The caseworker may contact people who know you and your family, have a lot of recommendations to help your family, and go with you to court, if necessary.

Your relationship with your caseworker is important. Try to be open with him or her about what you want and what you don't want. Your caseworker may not always be able to do what you want, but sometimes he or she can. Your caseworker can't do something you want unless he or she knows about it.

With some decisions you have to make in dealing with abuse issues, there may be no good choice at all. None of the choices is something you really want. A good caseworker will help you make these very hard decisions. You can also meet with your caseworker and therapist together to help with these decisions. It is important that you speak up about what you want to happen. Sometimes choosing the one that feels "least bad" is a way to have *some* control in your life. You don't have to be happy about hard choices, but it is good to know your ideas count.

Courts

If you have to go to court, it helps to be prepared. It will help if you talk with the lawyers and have time to ask plenty of questions. The lawyers or social workers should tell you things like what to expect, what the other lawyers will probably say, and what they think you'll need to talk about. They should explain things about the law, about what laws were broken and what you can do to help yourself. You should also have a chance to go inside the courtroom before the court date so you can see what it looks like. Even if the lawyer or caseworker doesn't offer to show you the courtroom, remember that you can ask them to.

Going to court is often a difficult experience, though some kids feel better afterwards. Some boys thought that having the chance to tell their stories out loud to a judge helped. And sometimes, telling the court can stop the abuser from abusing someone else in the future. These are very good reasons to do something that is hard.

Sometimes the abuser is found "not guilty" in a trial, or the case is called "unfounded" and the charges are dropped. This does not mean you were wrong to tell or that the judge did not believe you. Courts need certain facts that can be proved. This idea of proof may be easy in bank robberies, for instance. There may be witnesses, fingerprints, and even a videotape that recorded the whole thing. Sexual abuse is almost the opposite. If there were witnesses, they may be too scared or too mean, or they feel too guilty to say the truth about what they saw or participated in. There are no fingerprints and, usually, no physical proof to bring in front of the court. That's why sexual abuse can be hard to prove, and why people who have sexually abused others are sometimes not found guilty.

Relationship with the Abuser

Some boys have contact with the person who abused them, while some don't. Some boys want to have contact with the abuser and some don't. It's a very personal decision that depends on many things. If you *have* to see an abusive person because a court or parent says so, it's important for you to have other people whom you can trust present during the visit. It's also important that you *not* be alone with the abuser, something you might not be able to take care of on your own. If you end up alone with the person who abused you, then someone (the court, or your parent, or your caseworker) has probably let you down in a big way. Keep trying to find someone else who will help. If the abuser keeps touching you, keep telling.

People who sexually abuse children often say that they have changed and that they don't do that any more. Usually, that is more like wishful thinking than a real change. We know that, especially for adults, it takes a *long* time and a lot of help to change from wanting to sexually abuse to not wanting to sexually abuse. It usually takes many years and lots of hard work in special treatment programs. If your abuser says he or she has changed, it may be true, or it may just be the abuser's wishful thinking.

Be very careful with your feelings and your body, especially if you have contact with the person who abused you. Even if you like this person, it makes sense to be very careful around this person who has hurt you in the past. This relationship is very complicated. You may remember very caring times you had with him or her. The person may have been very kind in some ways. But if this person still has the inner desire to be sexual with you, it can be hard to protect yourself. You will need to be feeling very strong inside to be able to be close to the abuser AND protect yourself from any sneaky way he or she may try to be sexual. Remember, any person who should know better and behaves in a sexual way with a younger person or with someone who doesn't understand or want to be sexual has a BIG problem. It will take a long time for this person to change it.

Relationship with the World

Many things about being sexually abused are difficult, and you may feel bad or sad or angry about it even when you learn to feel good about yourself. But some of the results of sexual abuse can surprise you. Almost everyone has some bad experiences in his life. You probably know people who have experienced terrible things — like tornadoes, or going to jail unfairly, or being treated badly because of the color of their skin or because they have a serious birth defect. Some people become bitter and angry about these things. But many people choose to make good use of these bad experiences. They learn they had strengths they didn't know they had.

Many people who have been sexually abused have a deep understanding about certain truths. They really *know* that strong, innocent, good people get hurt. They know that people get hurt, and it's not their fault. They can become stronger people who stand up for truth and what's right in the world. They work to make society be fair to everyone. They want justice to be real. They often choose to use their power and courage to fight against cruelty. We hope you find some positive things about yourself and discover your strengths along your road to healing. We know that everyone has the power to make this happen.

School and Friends

Unless you decide to tell them, your friends and people at school probably won't know you've been sexually abused. It's not something that everyone needs to know. Sexual abuse is only one part of your life, and most likely that part will get less and less important as time goes by.

It's probably a good idea for you to think about who you want to know about what happened to you. It's good to have a few people you can count on to be able to talk to. A counselor or teacher at school that you trust might be a good person.

Also, it's natural to want to talk to people your own age. This can help a lot. But, it's also good to remember that sometimes kids can be curious about sexual things, but not always grown up enough to understand or to know how to help. It's a smart idea to do some good thinking when choosing friends to talk to about it.

It's possible that there is a group in your area where boys who have been sexually abused get together and talk with a therapist or counselor. Many boys find this helpful. If you are interested, tell your caseworker, therapist, parent, or another adult who is helping you. They may be able to help you find a group like this.

School and friends are a very important part of your life. If you are having trouble at school or with making friends, you can change it. The only person you can really change is yourself. Make it a part of your goals for yourself, and then get the help you need to do it. For example, if you think you'd make more friends if you were on a team, figure out what you need to do to try out. There are other teams besides baseball, football, and basketball. Try intramural teams or academic teams (chess or debate, for example). Try other things, such as golf, choir, theater groups or street hockey.

It sometimes happens, especially when the abuser is an older kid, that the abuser tells other people that he or she had sex with you. The people the abuser tells may approach you to have sex with them, too. They may threaten to tell other kids, call you names, or cause trouble for you. That is also abuse, and you need to tell your therapist, a guidance counselor, teacher, or your parents about it. Remember, sexual abuse is something that was done to you, you didn't ask for it or deserve it. The abuser is the one who should be ashamed. The best way to deal with threats and rumors is to stand up to them and hold your head up.

This may be a good time for you to think about your own reactions to the abuse and how they have affected your relationships with others. Do you have a hard time trusting anyone else? Have any of your close relationships with family members or friends changed since the abuse? Are you spending more time alone? Making excuses not to hang out with or talk to people you used to like?

If you're having trouble trusting or being close to others since the abuse, it's understandable. Many boys do. Their sense of trust was injured by the abuser and now they have this big awful secret. While being cautious about who to trust is wise, most kids (and adults) don't really feel good about themselves when they don't feel connected to other people.

On the other hand, does being alone feel too scary since the abuse? Do feelings and thoughts about the abuse come up when you're alone that you wish would go away? Are you finding excuses to hang out with people, ANY people, even people you wouldn't have wanted to hang out with before the abuse? To fit in with these people are you doing scary, dangerous things (like trying drugs or unprotected sex) to prove you're not scared?

Not wanting to be alone with scary feelings is a normal reaction to dealing with abuse. Another way to find friends is to join groups that do something you like to do or something you'd like to learn.

You can and should have good friends. Sometimes people who have been through very difficult experiences can make the best kind of friends if they *choose* to use their experiences to be more caring and understanding of other people. As a guideline, think about whether the person treats you and other people well, cares about what's best for you, and cares about himself or herself. How the person treats others, or talks about them when they're not around, is the same way he or she will treat you and talk about you.

The energy you use learning who to trust and how to make real friends will be well worth it. Make it a goal for yourself and get any help you need to make it work. You can do it. You can take hold of your life and get back on track.

Relationship with Yourself

Some boys find that a feeling or idea about the abuse comes back again after they thought it was over. If that happens for you, it doesn't mean there's a big problem — it just means that this idea or feeling needs more attention. Some guys keep having feelings about being "less of a man" because of the abuse. If questions about being less of a man come back to you, it just means you need to pay more attention, that this part needs more work. Find someone you can trust to talk to about it. Some guys try to "prove" how much of a man they are by being sexual a lot, or by acting tough and fighting all the time. But manhood, the quality of being a man, isn't something that can be taken away. It isn't something you have to prove. It is yours just by being alive, and most men realize that they don't have to prove it to anyone.

Remember, sexual abuse is a really hard thing for a lot of people. Some parts of healing take more time than others. Don't give up! People who have experienced sexual abuse in their lives can grow up to be kind, courageous, strong, and smart. You can choose to grow from hard times in your life.

Your Turn

Did your relationships with any friends or family members change after the abuse? List the family member and write down how the relationship changed.

_____

_____

_____

_____

_____

_____

If you want to have better relationships with friends or family but are having a hard time, write about why it's hard for you to trust others right now.

_____

_____

_____

_____

_____

_____

Write about some of the people you'd like to feel closer to and ways you might begin to learn if it is wise to trust them. What makes a person trustworthy? Are you trustworthy?

_____

_____

_____

_____

_____

_____

_____

_____

_____

_____

_____

_____

_____

Do you know anyone who had a really bad experience and learned something or found that something good came out of it? Write about that person.

Example

While growing up, Abe and his mother and sisters couldn't pay the rent after their father left. They spent several years without a place to call home. Abe remembers some nights at homeless shelters and even worse nights when the family could find no shelter at all. When Abe remembered the hard times his family went through, he wanted to help other families going through the same problems. Now as an adult, Abe volunteers his non-work time and his construction skills to Habitat for Humanity, an agency that helps build homes for people who would be unable to afford to own homes without this kind of help.

If you don't know any examples, ask people around you if they have ever learned something from a sad or bad experience.

Your example: _____

_____

_____

_____

_____

_____

_____

_____

What things have you learned so far from your experience of sexual abuse? Write about that and talk about it with a trusted person.

_____

_____

_____

_____

_____

_____

_____

What does being a man mean to you? Write about it.

_____

_____

_____

_____

_____

_____

_____

_____

Think of a man you like and respect. What do you like about him? How does he earn your respect? Describe him.

_____

_____

_____

_____

_____

_____

Think of yourself in 10 years. Write down how you would like someone to describe you.

_____

_____

_____

_____

_____

_____

_____

How will you get from here to be the person you want to be in 10 years? Think of what you need to do, what kind of help you might need, and who might give it to you. Write it down, and keep it in a safe place to look at every once in a while. See how much progress you are making toward your goals, or how they have changed.

Your Space

Staying on Track

Y, ou've probably already come a long way on your journey to getting your life back on the track that you want it to be on. Here are some of our ideas about what it takes to stay on track. Add lots of your own ideas too.

A Safe Place

The question, "Am I safe?" is a good one to ask yourself. Make a habit of asking yourself this question every once in awhile. What do we mean by safe? First of all, are you still in danger of being sexually, physically, or emotionally abused? If so, you are not safe and getting safe is what's important.

If you are unsure whether you are safe with a particular person or situation, it's important that you listen to your intuition or "gut feeling." Too often people don't listen to their inner warning bells (hunches or gut feelings) for reasons like not wanting to hurt anyone's feelings, not trusting their own inner sense, or thinking they're tough enough or smart enough to handle anything. And too often people get hurt this way. Listening to your intuition is one skill that can help you be safer. Of course, people's intuition is not always right. That's okay. It's better to make the safe choice.

While a big part of getting back on track is feeling more able to keep yourself safe, all kids need and deserve the help of adults to help them be safe. If you are unsure about your safety, tell someone until you hear very clearly that they will protect you. This person should also be able to answer your questions about how they will do this. You can re-read the section on "Some Ways to Find Help" in Chapter 1 for more ideas about how to get the help you need.

In some cases, a kid may feel so helpless that he leaves home and tries to run away to get safe. If you've considered running away, please don't. It's too dangerous. Many runaways don't escape sexual abuse, but run into more of it (by being raped or by being encouraged into prostitution — being a hooker or a hustler — as a way to make money to live). If you are in danger and need another place to stay, find a trusted adult to help you plan the best way to get to a safer place. There may be a shelter in your area especially for kids who need this kind of help.

Motivation

If only getting back on track had a short cut! For most people, healing takes lots of time and plenty of hard work. Motivation is the energy that keeps a person working towards something that they want. Being in the Olympics or being on the track team can motivate a person to keep training, exercising, and practicing, even when it means getting up early or jogging when it's cold and wet.

It takes a great deal of bravery and motivation to heal (what a relief, two things you already have!). Fortunately, getting back on track has many rewards, and it can actually be fun and exciting to learn and do things you never thought you could. Give yourself a pat on the back each time you make some progress. You deserve it.

Balance

Most of us can't work hard all the time. It's probably better for you if you can take some breaks to relax and have fun. Working at healing doesn't mean you can't enjoy life.

Sometimes boys who have been sexually abused spend so much of their energy trying to cope with what has happened, that they forget or never learn how to play and relax. If you think this has happened to you, talk to your therapist or other special helpers about it. If you want to, learning to have fun and discovering the things you like to do can be one of your goals of healing.

Special Helpers

Most people find the road to healing easier if they get the special help they need. This can come from several places — good relationships, special books, attention to our spiritual needs (faith in God and our religious beliefs), and therapy. You may find others. Take time to think about whether or not you have enough special helpers in your life. If not, tell this to someone who cares about you. Between the two of you, you can get more of what you need and deserve. And remember, all of your special helpers don't have to deal with sexual abuse. A good friend can do a lot to help you feel better, even if you choose not to talk about the abuse.

Other Strengths

Some kids grow up hearing about God and going to places to pray and learn about God, like a church, a synagogue, or a mosque. Even though it may not seem to help right away, lots of kids find that believing in things bigger than they are feels really good. If you were abused by a religious person, such as a priest, minister, Sunday school teacher, a rabbi, or a nun, it might feel more difficult to find extra strength in your religion for awhile. Try talking to someone else in your religious group about those feelings, and the difference between the God you worship and the people who abused you. If you've never prayed, you might give it a try, even if you don't belong to a religious group. Some people pray outdoors because being with trees or rivers or mountains helps them feel better. Some people don't think of the way they pray as talking to God, but as talking to the universe, or the stars, or a tree. Some people think of this as "turning over" their problems to something more powerful than they are. So if you have a problem and you've done everything you can to fix it, try to "turn it over" to God or the universe. It gives some people a peaceful and strong feeling.

Turning Your Life into Something Positive

Remember that some of the most courageous, wise and helpful people in the world had hurtful experiences in their childhood. They learned to take in new ideas and then find strength and courage.

Your Turn

If you picked a title for your life like it was a movie, what would the title be? What would you like the title to be when you are 21 years old? Write them both down here.

_____

_____

_____

_____

If the titles are different, write down here some things you can do to help make your life more like the second movie title. One thing might be, "Ask for help with my feelings when I need it."

_____

_____

_____

_____

_____

_____

_____

_____

_____

_____

Sometimes you read a book and it feels like, "Yup, that's just like me." Other times it feels like, "Nope, that's not me." It's good to think about how you feel — about books, about things that happen in your life, about people. Choose three of the best ideas in this book for you. Which ideas or feelings fit you best? Write them down here.

_____

_____

_____

_____

_____

What ideas do you wish we'd written more about? Which ideas do you disagree with? Write down some things you wish we'd talked about, talked more about, or that you disagreed with.

_____

_____

_____

_____

_____

We care a lot about whether this book helped you. We want to make it even better. If you want to share with us what you've written on these pages, make a copy and send it to Leslie Wright and Mindy Loiselle, *Back on Track*, Safer Society Press, P.O. Box 340, Brandon, VT 05733.

An Important Special Message

A note for anyone reading this book who is being sexually abused and no one knows yet . . .

TELL

TELL a teacher

TELL a police officer

TELL a relative

TELL a neighbor

TELL a friend's parent

TELL your parent . . .

Just keep telling until someone listens who STOPS the abuse. You will probably not be able to stop it by yourself. Abuse hurts people even if it doesn't feel like it right now. You may not always get the kind of help you want when you tell, but telling is the quickest way for abuse to stop, and the only way that an abuser might be stopped from hurting other kids.

Luís and the
Book of Hearing

Luís lived in an old brick house high up on a hill. In winter the house stayed warm as a winter sleeping bag on a cool summer night. In summer it stayed cool as a mountainside river. From his bedroom window, Luís could look down the hill to the beach far below. All through the year, the sea sang songs to the sand. Sometimes the sea whispered soft as the rustling leaves. Sometimes it boomed wild as a thunderstorm. Luís really loved to hear the sea sing!

Luís didn't have any brothers or sisters to play with him, but he had a mom and dad who loved him very much. All through the summer, they would go with Luís into the woods or down to the beach. There they would play games and sing silly songs and eat all kinds of wonderful foods from their picnic baskets.

In the fall and winter and spring, Luís would spend time with his friends in the school at the bottom of the hill. Luís had lots of friends, because he could run fast, jump high, and tell really funny jokes. He was pretty smart, too. And he lived in that great house on the hill, with a big yard right next to the woods. He also had a mom and dad who let him have lots of parties and sleepovers and campouts with his friends in the woods by the backyard all through the school year.

There was another boy at the school who didn't have so many friends. In fact he didn't seem to have *any* friends, as far as Luís could tell. Most all the boys and girls called him "Billy Bulldozer." No one quite seemed to know why. One day in the schoolyard, Luís asked his teammates if "Billy Bulldozer" was his real name, but Layne (the captain of the team) just laughed and said, "Who cares?"

Well, Luís *kind* of cared, but he didn't want to say so. He was afraid, you see, that the other boys might laugh at him, too. I bet you care, though, because you know that our names belong to us. No one should *ever* take away our names. So I'll tell you his real name: Tommy Ray. You and I, we'll keep calling him Tommy Ray, even if the others keep calling him Billy Bulldozer.

I bet you've known someone like Tommy Ray. He always went around with a silly smile on his face. He smiled even when the other kids made fun of him, or tripped him in the hall, or wouldn't let him play in their games. His clothes always looked a little dirty. Sometimes a *lot* dirty, when he wore the same shirt three or four days in a row. None of the kids seemed to like Tommy Ray. The teachers didn't even seem to like him. They looked the other way, most of the time, when someone played a trick on Tommy Ray.

Luís really did have a good heart. Deep down in his good heart he felt sorry for Tommy Ray (even if Luís *did* still call him Billy Bulldozer). Somehow he knew that Tommy Ray reminded all the girls and boys and the teachers of something they didn't want to think about. Luís didn't know what that "something" might be. He just knew that people got mad because Tommy Ray reminded them of it. He couldn't figure out what it all meant, so he just went along when the other kids played tricks on Tommy Ray.

Until the fall, that is, when he read the *Book of Hearing*. Then everything changed for him. Here's how it came about.

For science class that fall, Luís had to write a report on the ear. Late one afternoon, he rode his bike down the hill to the old brick library. Luís liked to go there because the library stood close to the sea. He could hear the sea, all the while he read books or did homework.

That afternoon, he flipped through the card catalog, looking for books about the ear. All at once, he came across a strange green-and-blue card (all the rest were white) with red letters. The card told him

about a book called the *Book of Hearing*. Luís thought that this book would be just what he needed, so he wrote down the call numbers (which are like your street address, only they tell us where to find a book in the library).

Luís didn't quite know where to start looking, so he went to the librarian's desk to ask for help. When he got there, he found a very old woman sitting behind the desk. Luís came to the library all the time, but he had never seen her before. He wondered why.

"Excuse me," he said politely. The very old woman looked up from the book in her hands. She didn't even smile at him. "I need to find this book," Luís said, just a little bit rattled by her stern look. The old woman took his slip of paper, still without smiling, looked down at it, then looked back at him. At last she smiled, a very very old smile.

"So you need to find the *Book of Hearing*," she said. Something about her words made Luís think of the songs of the sea.

"Yes ma'am," he answered. "For a report on the ear."

"A report on the ear?" the very old woman smiled. "Yes, yes. A report on the ear. Well, come with me."

Without another word, she rose from the desk. Luís followed her to a part of the library that he had never seen before. There she pulled a very big, very dusty old book from a top shelf. Handing it to Luís, she pointed to a stuffed chair in the corner.

"You can't take the *Book of Hearing* home with you," she rumbled soft as the sea in summer. "You'll have to read it here."

"Yes ma'am," Luís answered, as he crossed to the chair and sank into it.

Afterwards, Luís could never remember just *what* he read, or even when he left the library to go home. The whole time seemed a little bit like a dream to him. Just all at once, he found himself walking his bike up the hill to his house with the moon rising over the sea. He tried really hard to remember what he read in the *Book of Hearing* (he had to write his report on the ear, after all). But he just couldn't remember, no matter how hard he tried.

But then Luís noticed something really odd. Walking along with both hands on his handlebars, he seemed to be able to hear words in the song of the sea. In his ears the words sounded something like

> *Soft song of the sea*
>
> *Singing to the sand*
>
> *Soft song of the sky*
>
> *Singing to the land*

Turning his head this way and that, Luís found that he could hear the wind talking to the trees, the birds scolding the chipmunks, the creek telling secrets to the ferns. Never in his life had he heard so many songs and so much soft chatter! That night, long after he should have been asleep, Luís lay awake to hear the night songs.

The next morning, a little bit sleepy, he grabbed his lunch, kissed his mom and dad, then jumped onto his bike to go to school. All the way down the hill, he heard all the wonderful songs of the world that he had never heard before.

But when he got to the bottom of the hill, he heard a new song that really wasn't a song at all. It came from very far away. It sounded very sad, as sad as a puppy that someone kicked really hard. Forgetting about school, Luís followed the sound of the song along paths and backroads. At last he came to an ugly little house in an ugly little yard. The sad song came from this house.

Leaning his bike against the broken gate, Luís slipped up to a window with one pane cracked. Through the window he saw a little broken table in a very messy kitchen. And then he saw someone standing there — it was Tommy Ray (even though Luís *did* still call him Billy Bulldozer). While Luís watched through the window, Tommy Ray took two slices of stiff white bread, spread them with mustard from a crusty jar on the table, sprinkled the mustard with some sugar, smushed the two pieces of bread together, then stuffed the sandwich into a crumpled brown paper bag.

Every couple of minutes a man came stomping through the kitchen. Luís guessed that he must be Tommy Ray's dad. Whenever the man walked by Tommy Ray, he smacked the little boy on the back of the head. Now Luís saw no reason for the smacks, no reason at all. After all, Tommy Ray was only standing there making his mustard-and-sugar sandwich. So Luís figured that the man just didn't like Tommy Ray, the way the boys and girls and the teachers didn't like him.

Watching at the window, Luís saw that Tommy Ray scrunched his face and hunched his shoulders whenever the man walked by. Luís figured that Tommy Ray must know that another smack would be coming his way. All the while, that silly, sad smile stayed on Tommy Ray's face.

Turning from the window, Luís went to his bike then rode on to school. All the way there, he heard the new songs of birds taking flight, puppies romping, and Tommy Ray walking out his ugly little house with his mustard-and-sugar sandwich in the brown paper bag clutched in his hand.

All that morning, Luís tried really hard to pay attention to his lessons, but he kept hearing the soft sad song that swirled around Tommy Ray (even though Luís *did* still call him Billy Bulldozer). He wondered why no one else could hear it. There Tommy Ray sat, at the back of the class. That silly smile never left his face. A crumpled brown bag sat on the edge of his desk. All through the morning, Luís wished many times that he didn't know what was in the that bag.

At last the morning ended. Recess came, then social studies, then lunch. Luís had a fine big lunch, packed by his mom and dad. His lunchbox held two heaping sandwiches on good brown bread, cheese and grapes, some carrot and celery sticks, a carton of orange juice, three cupcakes and a small bag of cookies. Grabbing his lunch from his desk, he went to join his friends in the lunchroom.

Walking into the lunchroom, Luís saw all his best friends sitting around a table near the middle of the room. He started to walk toward them. He could hear their great bubbling song of laughter. All at once, though, Luís stopped still as a garden statue. The soft sad song he had heard all morning seemed sadder here in the lunchroom.

Looking around, Luís saw Tommy Ray sitting alone at a table far at the back of the room. He still had that silly smile on his face. He had torn his mustard-and-sugar sandwich in half. The two halves lay on the crumpled brown bag in front of him. Luís saw Tommy Ray staring at the sandwich, as though he didn't quite know what it might be. And *still* that silly smile. Luís *hated* that silly smile!

All around him Luís heard the happy songs of the other kids. He also heard ugly songs something like frogs croaking. He knew the croakings must be the songs of the kids making fun of Tommy Ray. Somehow these croakings grew louder and louder, until Luís could hardly hear anything else.

And then Luís's ears did the most wonderful thing. They stopped hearing all the ugly croakings. Instead they heard only the soft sad song coming from the table where a boy sat alone, a boy who had to

eat mustard-and-sugar sandwiches, a boy who got smacked for no reason, a boy whose real name no one even remembered. Standing there in the lunchroom, his great good lunch in his hand, Luís remembered a time he thought he had forgotten forever.

Luís hadn't always lived in an old brick house on a hill, with a mom and dad who loved him very very much. He had been born in a land far away. In that far-away place, people got killed in wars all the time. Little boys and girls often had no mom or dad at all because they had been killed, even when they hadn't been in the fighting or done anything wrong. Luís had been one of those little boys, kicked here and kicked there. Sometimes he had to eat whatever he could find in the streets, even moldy bread and other people's garbage. Many, many bad things had been done to him. But at last he came to live in the old brick house on a hill. There he found a new mom and dad who loved him very very much. After a long time Luís forgot about that other place.

Until that day when he stood in the lunchroom, looking at a table in the back where Tommy Ray sat alone with a mustard-and-sugar sandwich torn in half.

Luís turned and smiled to his friends. They looked a little bit puzzled, because Luís didn't seem to hear them calling him to come sit with them. Then they saw Luís begin to walk toward the back of the lunchroom. Everyone in the whole room got quiet when they saw — could it *really* be? — that Luís was walking toward Billy Bulldozer's table! No one could think of a word to say when Luís stopped in front of Billy Bulldozer! At first no one even knew who had spoken when they heard,

"Hey Billy. Mind if I sit down?"

Of course it was Luís who had spoken. He felt very sad when he saw that the other boy had scrunched his face and hunched his shoulders, just like he did when his dad smacked him.

"Billy," Luís said again. "Okay if I sit down?"

"It's Tommy Ray," the other boy said, so softly that Luís hardly heard him.

"What?" Luís asked.

"It's Tommy Ray," the other boy said again, louder this time. "My name's *Tommy Ray.*"

All at once, Luís heard the crashing of a great rushing river. He thought that all the waters of the world must have gathered in one place. He whirled around to look at the lunchroom, but he could see no rushing river at all. He whirled back to Tommy Ray. Then Luís saw that one single little tear had trickled from Tommy Ray's eye. He also saw that the silly smile had left Tommy Ray's face at last.

"Okay Tommy Ray," he smiled. "My name's Luís. Mind if I sit down?"

"If you want," was all Tommy Ray said.

Not hearing the whispers and giggles and even shouts, Luís ate lunch that day with Tommy Ray. In the way that some kids know such things, Luís knew he shouldn't just *give* part of his lunch to Tommy Ray. Instead he groaned about how *full* he was, and how he *hated* to waste food. Then he asked if Tommy Ray would mind helping him eat all this food, so Luís wouldn't feel bad about wasting it. Tommy Ray said he wouldn't mind helping.

Luís never knew why, but right after that first lunch with Tommy Ray, his ears stopped hearing the words to the songs of the sea and the wind and the woods. But his heart still heard them, and he knew that was good enough. After that first lunch, Luís and Tommy Ray shared many lunches. In no time at all they became best friends.

All these things happened long ago. Both Luís and Tommy Ray are grown up now, with little boys of their own. They're still best friends.

Luís never again saw the very old woman with the very old smile. Many times he looked for the *Book of Hearing*, but he never found it again. He sometimes came across books that were *something* like it. Or at least, they seemed like they *might* be a part of it. After a while, Luís decided that the *Book of Hearing* must have fallen apart, and he would have to look in many places to find it all again.

And here you've found a part of it, and you can tell others who might need to find the *Book of Hearing*.

David Calof, Editor Emeritus
Treating Abuse Today
Seattle, Washington

Select Safer Society Publications

STOP! Just for Kids: For Kids with Sexual Touching Problems Adapted by Terri Allred and Gerald Burns (1997) $15.

A Primer on the Complexities of Traumatic Memories of Childhood Sexual Abuse: A Psychobiological Approach by Fay Honey Knopp & Anna Rose Benson (1997) $25.

The Last Secret: Daughters Sexually Abused by Mothers by Bobbie Rosencrans (1997) $20.

Shining Through: Pulling It Together After Sexual Abuse REVISED EDITION by Mindy Loiselle and Leslie Bailey Wright (1997). $14. For girls aged 10 and up. New material on body image, self-esteem, self-talk, and sexuality.

37 to One: Living as an Integrated Multiple by Phoenix J. Hocking (1996). $12.00.

The Brother / Sister Hurt: Recognizing the Effects of Sibling Abuse by Vernon Wiehe, Ph.D. (1996) $10.00.

Men & Anger: Understanding and Managing Your Anger for a Much Better Life by Murray Cullen & Rob Freeman-Longo. Revised and updated, new self-esteem chapter. (1996). $15.00.

When Children Abuse: Group Treatment Strategies for Children with Impulse Control Problems by Carolyn Cunningham and Kee MacFarlane. Incorporates and updates their well-respected previous volume *When Children Molest Children,* adding new material on medications, shame and entitlement, firesetting, and animal abuse. (1996). $28.00.

Adult Sex Offender Assessment Packet by Mark Carich & Donya Adkerson (1995). $8.00.

Empathy and Compassionate Action: Issues & Exercises: A Workbook for Clients in Treatment by Robert Freeman-Longo, Laren Bays, & Euan Bear (1995). $12.00.

The Difficult Connection: The Therapeutic Relationship in Sex Offender Treatment by Geral T. Blanchard (1995). $10.00.

From Trauma to Understanding: A Guide for Parents of Children with Sexual Behavior Problems by William D. Pithers, Alison S. Gray, Carolyn Cunningham, & Sandy Lane (1993). $5.00.

Adolescent Sexual Offender Assessment Packet by Alison Stickrod Gray & Randy Wallace (1992). $8.00.

The Relapse Prevention Workbook for Youth in Treatment by Charlene Steen (1993). $15.00.

Pathways: A Guided Workbook for Youth Beginning Treatment by Timothy J. Kahn (Revised 1996). $15.00.

Pathways Guide for Parents of Youth Beginning Treatment by Timothy J. Kahn (Revised 1997). $8.00.

Man-to-Man, When Your Partner Says NO: Pressured Sex & Date Rape by Scott Allen Johnson (1992). $6.50.

When Your Wife Says No: Forced Sex in Marriage by Fay Honey Knopp (1994). $7.00.

Female Adolescent Sexual Abusers: An Exploratory Study of Mother-Daughter Dynamics with Implications for Treatment by Marcia T. Turner & Tracey N. Turner (1994). $18.00.

Who Am I & Why Am I in Treatment? A Guided Workbook for Clients in Evaluation and Beginning Treatment by Robert Freeman-Longo & Laren Bays (1988; 7th printing). $12.00.

Why Did I Do It Again? Understanding My Cycle of Problem Behaviors by Laren Bays & Robert Freeman-Longo (1989; 5th printing). $12.00.

How Can I Stop? Breaking My Deviant Cycle by Laren Bays, Robert Freeman-Longo, & Diane Hildebran (1990; 4th printing). $12.00.

Adults Molested As Children: A Survivor's Manual for Women & Men by Euan Bear with Peter Dimock (1988; 4th printing). $12.95.

Family Fallout: A Handbook for Families of Adult Sexual Abuse Survivors by Dorothy Beaulieu Landry, M.Ed. (1991). $12.95.

Embodying Healing: Integrating Bodywork and Psychotherapy in Recovery from Childhood Sexual Abuse by Robert J. Timms, Ph.D., and Patrick Connors, C.M.T. (1992). $15.00.

The Safer Society Press publishes additional books, audiocassettes, and training videos related to the treatment of sexual abuse. For a catalog of our complete listings, please check the box on the order form (next page).

Order Form

Date _____

Shipping Address

☐ *Please send a catalog.*

Name and/or Agency _____

Street Address _____
(NO PO BOX)
_____

City _____ State _____ Zip _____

Billing Address *(IF DIFFERENT FROM SHIPPING ADDRESS)*

Address _____

City _____ State _____ Zip _____

Purchase Order # _____

Visa or MasterCard # _____ Exp. Date _____

Signature _____

Daytime Phone (_____) _____

QTY	TITLE #	TITLE	UNIT PRICE	TOTAL COST
		SUBTOTAL		
		VT RESIDENTS ADD SALES TAX		
		SHIPPING *(SEE BELOW)*		
		TOTAL		

*All orders must
be prepaid.*

Make checks payable to:
SAFER SOCIETY PRESS.

**All prices subject to change
without notice.**

NO RETURNS

Mail to:

PO BOX 340 • BRANDON, VERMONT 05733-0340

Phone: (802) 247-3132

Shipping:
• **1–9 items add $5 shipping.**
• **10 or more items add 8% shipping.**
• **Rush Order add $10 and call for
  actual shipping costs.**

Bulk discounts available:
Please inquire.